T0291418

Cultural Proximity and Organization

Cultural proximity consists of shared language, codes, and norms of communication and exchange between actors. It is generally considered important for organizations, enhancing communication and facilitation interaction between actors. In such situations, diversity is often seen as a source of richness and originality. However, high levels of proximity might create some risk, leading to lock-in and inertia, with a negative impact on the innovativeness of the organization.

While the role of cultural proximity is subject to much debate within organizations studies, a comprehensive understanding of cultural proximity remains elusive. This book explores the organizational implications of the concept of cultural proximity, delving into the managerial challenges posed by diversities and similarities in culture within a business environment using different levels of analysis. The key messages of the present book, grounded on original empirical evidence, can be summarized as follows: cultural proximity is a key factor for managing innovation in present times; innovation requires a deliberate orchestration of the dichotomy between cultural proximity/cultural diversity; there are specific circumstances where proximity can be beneficial for managers and entrepreneurs.

The book will be of value to researchers, academics, managers, and students in the fields of management science, human resource management, innovation studies, and organizational studies.

Federica Ceci is an Associate Professor of Innovation Management in the Department of Business Administration at the University G. d'Annunzio, Italy.

Francesca Masciarelli is an Associate Professor of Management and Entrepreneurship in the Business and Economics Department at University G. d'Annunzio, Italy.

Routledge Focus on Business and Management

The fields of business and management have grown exponentially as areas of research and education. This growth presents challenges for readers trying to keep up with the latest important insights. Routledge Focus on Business and Management presents small books on big topics and how they intersect with the world of business research.

Individually, each title in the series provides coverage of a key academic topic, whilst collectively, the series forms a comprehensive collection across the business disciplines.

Global Entrepreneurship Analytics
Using GEM Data
Milenka Linneth Argote Cusi and León Darío Parra Bernal

The Customer Experience Model
Adyl Aliekperov

Organizational Justice and Organizational Change
Managing By Love
Dominique A. David

Cultural Proximity and Organization
Managing Diversity and Innovation
Federica Ceci and Francesca Masciarelli

Entrepreneurial Urban Regeneration
Business Improvement Districts as a Form of Organizational Innovation
Rezart Prifti and Fatma Jaupi

For more information about this series, please visit: www.routledge.com/Routledge-Focus-on-Business-and-Management/book-series/FBM

Cultural Proximity and Organization

Managing Diversity and Innovation

**Federica Ceci and
Francesca Masciarelli**

Routledge
Taylor & Francis Group

NEW YORK AND LONDON

First published 2021
by Routledge
52 Vanderbilt Avenue, New York, NY 10017

and by Routledge
2 Park Square, Milton Park, Abingdon, Oxon, OX14 4RN

Routledge is an imprint of the Taylor & Francis Group, an informa business

© 2021 Taylor & Francis

Library of Congress Cataloging-in-Publication Data
Names: Ceci, Federica, author. | Masciarelli, Francesca,
author.
Title: Cultural proximity and organization : managing
diversity and innovation / Federica Ceci and Francesca
Masciarelli.
Description: New York, NY : Routledge, 2021. |
Series: Routledge focus on business and management |
Includes bibliographical references and index.
Identifiers: LCCN 2020021906 | ISBN 9780367513160 (hardback) |
ISBN 9781003053347 (ebook)
Subjects: LCSH: Diversity in the workplace. |
Social capital (Sociology)
Classification: LCC HF5549.5.M5 C43 2021 |
DDC 658.3008—dc23
LC record available at https://lccn.loc.gov/2020021906

ISBN: 978-0-367-51316-0 (hbk)
ISBN: 978-1-003-05334-7 (ebk)

Typeset in Times New Roman
by codeMantra

Contents

Introduction

In a world where the business environment is shaped by the two opposite forces of deglobalization and globalization, a reflection upon the role of culture and cultural proximity within organizations is compelling. This book represents an attempt to open the black box of cultural proximity, that is, shared language, codes and norms of communication, and exchange between actors, and it explores the connection between cultural proximity and innovation processes. Based on original empirical evidence coming from survey and case studies, and by means of multiple theoretical lenses from a variety of fields (sociology, management, and economy), we deeply investigate the concept of cultural proximity, its role in influencing innovative performance in organizations, discussing its benefits and limits, and providing implications for managers and policymakers.

In fact, while proximity is generally considered essential for organizations promoting communication and facilitating interaction between actors (Batjargal, 2003; Sajuria, vanHeerde-Hudson, Hudson, Dasandi, & Theocharis, 2015; Vissa, 2012; Williams, 2006), too much proximity might lead to lock-in and inertia (Gargiulo & Benassi, 2000; Grabher, 1993; Laursen, Masciarelli, & Prencipe, 2012; McPherson, Smith-Lovin, & Cook, 2001; Smith, Smith, & Shaw, 2017; Uzzi, 1997). The role of proximity is widely debated within organization studies; however, there is still a need for a comprehensive understanding of cultural proximity. Building on original empirical evidence, this book provides a new framework on cultural proximity, discussing the role of cultural proximity both within and outside the organizations, and exploring the managerial challenges posed by cultural diversities and similarities within a business environment.

The book is structured in two parts, each part contributing to the debate from a distinctive perspective: theoretical the first and empirical the second. This is intended to provide a global understanding of the phenomenon. In fact, to our knowledge, there are no published academic studies that provide a theoretical/analytical/empirical basis for the effects of cultural proximity on organizations.

Preview of the Message in the Present Book

The key messages of the present book can be summarized using an index card (see Figure I.1) as follows:

1   Cultural proximity is a key factor for managing innovation in present times.
2   Innovation requires a deliberate orchestration of the dichotomy between cultural proximity/cultural heterogeneity.
3   There are specific circumstances where cultural proximity can be beneficial for managers and entrepreneurs, and these will be illustrated.

Case Study: The Evolution of a Cultural Network Based on Cultural Proximity

The three messages of the book as presented above also emerge from the following case study. The case study is based on the longitudinal analysis of the evolution of an Association (which we prefer to keep anonymous) of entrepreneurs, characterized by shared culture and values within the network. As will be discussed, the cultural proximity existing in the group of entrepreneurs enabled the creation and functioning of an Association based on shared values that facilitated innovation through (i) knowledge sharing (Ceci & Prencipe, 2019), (ii) learning of the entrepreneurs involved in the network (Ceci, Masciarelli, & Prencipe, 2016), and (iii) implementation of innovative ideas (Ceci, Masciarelli, & Poledrini, 2019).

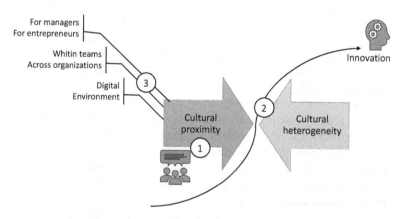

Figure I.1 An index card-sized preview of the book.

The Association was founded in 1985, but fully developed in the early 1990s. At the time, the founding members meet every 15 days. In the words of one of the founding members interviewed:

> I remember that some friends and me left at three, three and a half in the morning, once by train, once by car, to join the meetings, which were basically working meetings held on Saturday morning. It was a precious time; we had the opportunity to share a lot. We used to discuss about values, experiences, ideas. That path lasted several years, and it created a basis for what characterizes the Association today.

The activities of the Association began as a network of entrepreneurs and managers who wanted to share human and economic resources for mutual benefit. Currently, the Association has 38 branches in Italy, 17 abroad, and counts over 36,000 members. The main objective of the Association is to promote and develop relationships among its members. It offers its members services such as commercial and financial agreements, training activities, support for international business, job creation, and innovation. The Association is structured in national and local branches. Local branches are strongly connected to their territory and are therefore very different from each other. Although local branches present differences in the organization, they share the same culture, beliefs, as well as the same methodology for doing business, as one of our interviewees reported:

> In the first few years, it was an extraordinary experience since we worked a lot on ideas, with the aim of looking at the person and his or her needs. The person is linked to the organization and not separated from it. This idea is the fundamental belief that governs our association.

Sharing this idea allowed members to put their efforts together in building a common dream: an association that could help entrepreneurs and their organizations to thrive in the market, providing job opportunities to employees and positive effects on the territory. Sharing a common dream enabled the entrepreneurs in the network to share their knowledge, pool their resources, and develop projects together in order to innovate and be competitive in the market. The time that is spent together fosters the creation of a cultural proximity that is not based on past experience, nor on a territorial heritage (entrepreneurs used to travel to meet each other), but is based on shared values and norms build together over time. Therefore, we can affirm that cultural proximity can span over time and space, making it a form of proximity appropriate to the present time that is characterized by a lack of physical distance (Key Message n. 1).

In the following years (i.e. the 1990s), the efforts of the Association focused on the development of services for members, such as banking conventions, low internet and phone rates, and consultancy. This worked well for a while, until the mid-2000s, when, according to one interviewee, *"The world changed radically. In the following years we reconsidered the real meaning of being part of a network and we adapted the activities of the Association to the changing times."* Members realized that what the Association offered was not enough to innovate and survive in the market, therefore they decided to give rise a series of initiatives aimed at facilitating the exchange of ideas, knowledge, and opportunities, even with entrepreneurs and organizations outside the network, that is, more distant from a cultural viewpoint. The Association planned a series of networking events and fostered collaborations with other firm networks, far from their values and beliefs. One interviewee said

> Practically, this is how the Association has changed to mirror the changed reality. Today it is no longer an Association providing services, although some services are still being offered, but it has increasingly entered into the core business of the company, without taking the place of the entrepreneur. Today, the Association creates opportunities to enlarge the relationships and possibilities of its members.

An example of these initiatives is the 'Business Aid Group', a group of entrepreneurs who, having gone through a crisis, decided to help other entrepreneurs facing difficulties, to support them, and help them for free. As described in the interviews, this group, comprising ten entrepreneurs, meets the entrepreneur in difficulty, listens to him, and tries to find a solution, often bringing him in contact with other realities, both national and international ones. They try to find partners for ideas or new business opportunities. This experience highlights the importance of the balance between cultural proximity and heterogeneity in innovation. In the rest of the book this dichotomy will be discussed in greater detail but, even in this preliminary case study, we can see that members of a network characterized by high cultural proximity, consider the opportunity to exchange ideas and businesses with entrepreneurs having lower cultural proximity in order to foster innovation and solve a business crisis (Key Message n.2). This short case also shows that that different situations and different actors require an appropriate cultural proximity management that can be advantageous in some situations (e.g. a more stable environment?) and detrimental in others (e.g. rapid and unexpected changes?) (Key Message n.3). The present book aims to address these issues through a theoretical as well as an empirical approach.

How the Present Book Is Structured

The book is structured in two main parts and includes six chapters, as illustrated in Figure I.2. The first part, that is, Chapters 1–3, focuses on the main theoretical approaches that we believe fundamental to define and study cultural proximity. In this part,

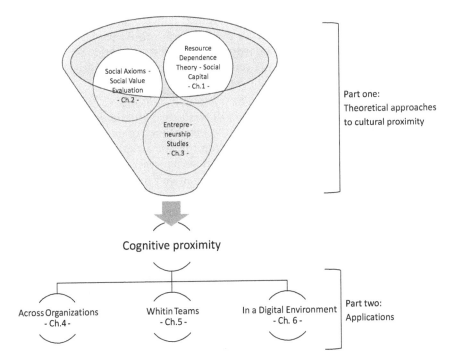

Figure I.2 Organization of the book.

we describe and discuss theories from a sociological, managerial, and economic point of view. We discuss the main gaps in these theories, and we highlight their contribution to the field of innovation management. The second part of the book, that is Chapters 4–6, is built upon empirical evidence delving deeply into the role of proximity in different contexts: inside an organization, within groups and teams, and in the digital environment.

Part One: Theoretical Approaches to Cultural Proximity

1   *Social capital theory and its application in innovation studies: a theoretical primer*

In this chapter, we will discuss the Resource Dependence Theory as a possible conceptual framework to investigate cultural proximity. The Resource Dependence Theory highlights the importance of external forces for firms when they prepare to compete in their environment (Pfeffer & Salancik, 1978). Directly stemming from the Resource Dependence Theory, the Social Capital Theory complements this vision (Portes, 1998). It represents an essential theoretical lens to analyze the relationships and assets of an organization rooted in those relationships, such as solidarity, trusts, and trustworthiness. The chapter will provide an overview of the two theories, discussing their implication for innovation management.

2   *Cultural dimensions, social axioms, and cultural proximity*

In the second chapter, we will further explore the research on cultural values, underlining the importance of cultural agreement for organizations. Based on the Social Value Evaluation theory, we discuss how organizations address incompatibilities in team members' beliefs and normative expectations. Incompatibilities might affect their ability to coordinate tasks, thus having a negative effect on organizations' performance (Denison & Mishra, 1995; Weber & Camerer, 2003). However, when the members of an organization are granted access to a broad array of cultural resources, the organization may have a greater capacity for creativity and innovation to follow changes, uncertainty, and competition for environmental demands (Feldman & Orlikowski, 2011; Friedland, 2012; Stark, Beunza, Girard, & Lukács, 2011). Based on this debate, we will summarize such theoretical positions, highlighting their implications for scholars and practitioners.

3   *Entrepreneurship and cultural proximity*
   In the third chapter, we will focus on the specific role that cultural proximity can play for innovative entrepreneurs. Deviating from the Upper Echelons Theory that suggests that organizational outcomes, strategic choice, and performance levels are affected by the entrepreneur's past experience and personal characteristics (Hambrick & Mason, 1984), we will discuss how entrepreneurs' personal beliefs determine the way external information, conditions, and stimuli are filtered, interpreted, and incorporated into decisions. In this context, cultural proximity refers to the similarity in the perceptions, interpretations, understanding, and evaluations that actors have of the world. Furthermore, it increases the likelihood of inter-organizational collaboration since it reduces the cognitive distance between partnering organizations looking for mutual benefits, and it provides identities for organizations searching for exchange partners. The role of cultural proximity in entrepreneurial networks will be discussed in detail.

Part Two: Applications

4   *Proximity outside organizations: a study on inter-organization networks*
   The second part of the book is based on empirical data, case studies, and survey data. Chapter 4 will analyze the results of a case study conducted in a cultural network of entrepreneurs. Being part of a network of individuals having similar norms, principles, and values has a strong impact on personal and business behavior; the resulting social networks are characterized by a great sense of identity between members, social support, and the presence of shared frameworks for the interpretation of reality. Shared values promote idea exchange, opportunity identification, and resource and knowledge combination by a wide and heterogeneous range of actors. This chapter will look into the benefits and shortcomings of this network configuration.

5   *Proximity within organizations: evidences from teams*
   Chapter 5 will explore the dynamics of cultural proximity within a team, investigating the role of culture and social value inside the team. Several psychological studies have explored, classified, and evaluated personal value: in this chapter we will use the construct of social axioms as a way of thinking,

describing, and measuring culture (Leung and Bond, 2004). Social axioms as "generalized beliefs about oneself, the social and physical environment" (Leung et al., 2002, p. 289). The concept of social axiom is intended to provide a cognitive interpretation of how individuals relate to others and their environment, and to investigate the relevance of beliefs in different social contexts. Starting from original survey data, a model of social value evaluation is constructed to explore the interaction between the heterogeneity of cultural characteristics in teams and team performance.

6 *The evolution of proximity: the impact of the digital revolution*

This chapter will investigate the challenges that digitalization poses to communication both within and outside organizations. Actors may interact virtually by means of information technology or they may communicate through face-to-face interactions. The latter have been proved to have a crucial role in fostering economic activities since they enable the development of shared values and a common vision. However, the recent technological progress has boosted collaborations and interactions between people living and working in different places. Therefore, people working within the same company are also called to collaborate and communicate using ICT tools. This chapter provides a contribution to the debate exploring the effect that ICT-based interactions have on innovative activities, and the moderating role played by cultural proximity. Furthermore, the chapter will clarify the circumstances under which such interactions are more effective, as well as the specific implications for scholars and practitioners.

Methodological Appendix

In order to collect the data to explore the research questions described so far, we conducted a preliminary study on the innovation dynamics occurring in a local branch of the Association, collecting 23 interviews, 14 with general managers or CEOs and nine with those responsible for other functions (e.g. sales, finance, production, marketing) (Ceci et al., 2019). In September and October 2014, we conducted 10 open-ended interviews, with key informants associated to the Association. The complete list of the interviewees can be found in Table I.1. the questionnaire used aimed at understanding the critical values that guide the entrepreneurial vision and how these values are shared within the cultural network.

Table I.1 List of interviews

Exploratory interviews	Date	Time	Length	Role within the association
E1	16/10/12	16:00	33'	President of the local branch
E2	16/10/12	17:00	45'	Former president of the local branch

Interview no.	Date	Time	Length	Firm	Role within the firm
1	26/11/12	09:15	34'	Rho	Finance and administration
2	26/11/12	10:00	33'	Beta	Ceo
3	26/11/12	11:30	30'	Phi	Ceo
4	26/11/12	12:00	37'	Zeta	Ceo
5	26/11/12	14:00	26'	Ni	Ceo
6	26/11/12	15:45	48'	Delta	Ceo
7	26/11/12	16:30	26'	Upsilon	Ceo
8	26/11/12	18:00	27'	Sigma	Ceo
9	27/11/12	10:40	20'	Iota	Sales manager
10	27/11/12	11:35	25'	Alpha	Ceo
11	27/11/12	12:30	24'	Xi	Ceo
12	27/11/12	14:00	26'	Omicron	Software developer
13	27/11/12	15:00	54'	Pi	Sales manager
14	27/11/12	17:00	24'	Chi	Sales director
15	27/11/12	17:30	30'	Gamma	Marketing manager
16	27/11/12	18:00	30'	Epsilon	Ceo
17	28/11/12	09:30	60'	Psi	Ceo
18	28/11/12	11:00	45'	Tau	Ceo
19	28/11/12	11:50	17'	Theta	Sales manager
20	28/11/12	12:20	20'	Eta	Production manager
21	28/11/12	14:00	38'	Kappa	Ceo
22	28/11/12	15:20	15'	Lambda	Ceo
23	28/11/12	16:00	24'	Mu	Sales director

Follow up interviews	Date	Time	Length	Role within the association
F1	18/9/14	e-mail		Member of the board of directors of a local branch
F2	19/9/14	10:00	30'	President of a local branch
F3	24/9/14	10:00	34'	Member of the board of directors of the association
F4	25/9/14	11:00	23'	–
F5	29/9/14	12:00	17'	Member of the board of directors of a local branch
F6	30/9/14	11:00	50'	President of the local branch
F7	1/10/14	10:30	15'	–
F8	3/10/14	11:45	9'	President of the local branch
F9	3/10/14	15:30	24'	Member of the board of directors of the association
F10	15/10/14	10:00	10'	–

References

Batjargal, B. (2003). Social capital and entrepreneurial performance in Russia: A longitudinal study. *Organization Studies (01708406), 24*(4), 535–556.

Ceci, F., Masciarelli, F., & Poledrini, S. (2019). How social capital affects innovation in a cultural network: Exploring the role of bonding and bridging social capital. *European Journal of Innovation Management.* [Ahead-of-Print].

Ceci, F., Masciarelli, F., & Prencipe, A. (2016). Entrepreneurial learning in a network: The role of cultural values. In Passiante G. & Romano A. *Creating Technology-Driven Entrepreneurship* (pp. 221–240). Palgrave Macmillan, London Springer.

Ceci, F., & Prencipe, A. (2019). Is there a supreme being controlling the universe? Entrepreneurs' personal beliefs and their impact on network learning. *International Journal of Entrepreneurship and Small Business, 38*(3), 359–378.

Denison, D. R., & Mishra, A. K. (1995). Toward a theory of organizational culture and effectiveness. *Organization Science, 6*(2), 204–223.

Feldman, M. S., & Orlikowski, W. J. (2011). Theorizing practice and practicing theory. *Organization Science, 22*, 1240–1253.

Friedland, R. (2012). The institutional logics perspective: A new approach to culture, structure, and process. *M@n@gement, 15*(5), 583.

Gargiulo, M., & Benassi, M. (2000). Trapped in your own net? Network cohesion, structural holes, and the adaptation of social capital. *Organization Science, 11*(2), 183–196.

Grabher, G. (1993). The weakness of strong ties. The lock-in of regional developmente in the Ruhr area. In G. Grabher (Ed.), *The embedded firm* (pp. 255–277). London and New York: Routledge.

Hambrick, D. C., & Mason, P. A. (1984). Upper echelon: The organization as a reflection if its top managers. *Academy of Management Review, 9*, 193–206.

Laursen, K., Masciarelli, F., & Prencipe, A. (2012). Trapped or spurred by the home region? The effects of potential social capital on involvement in foreign markets for goods and technology. *Journal of International Business Studies, 43*, 783–807.

Leung, K., Bond, M. H., Reimel de Carrasquel, S., Muñoz, C., Hernández, M., & Murakami, F. (2002). Social axioms: The search for universal dimensions of general beliefs about how the world functions. *Journal of Cross- Cultural Psychology, 33*, 286–302.

Leung, K., & Bond, M. H. (2004). Social Axioms: A Model for Social Beliefs in Multicultural Perspective. In M. P. Zanna (Ed.), *Advances in Experimental Social Psychology* (Vol. 36, pp. 119–197). Elsevier Academic Press.

McPherson, M., Smith-Lovin, L., & Cook, J. M. (2001). Birds of a feather: Homophily in social networks. *Annual Review of Sociology, 27*(1), 415–444.

Pfeffer, J., & Salancik, G. R. (1978). *The external control of organizations.* New York: Harper and Row.

Portes, A. (1998). Social capital: Its origins and applications in modern sociology. *Annual Review of Sociology, 24,* 1–24.

Sajuria, J., vanHeerde-Hudson, J., Hudson, D., Dasandi, N., & Theocharis, Y. (2015). Tweeting alone? An analysis of bridging and bonding social capital in online networks. *American Politics Research, 43*(4), 708–738.

Smith, C., Smith, J. B., & Shaw, E. (2017). Embracing digital networks: Entrepreneurs' social capital online. *Journal of Business Venturing, 32*(1), 18–34.

Stark, D., Beunza, D., Girard, M., & Lukács, J. (2011). *The sense of dissonance: Accounts of worth in economic life.* Princeton University Press, 2011.

Uzzi, B. (1997). Social structure and competition in interfirm networks: The paradox of embeddedness. *Administrative Science Quarterly, 42,* 35–67.

Vissa, B. (2012). Agency in action: Entrepreneurs' networking style and initiation of economic exchange. *Organization Science, 23*(2), 492–510.

Weber, R. A., & Camerer, C. F. (2003). Cultural conflict and merger failure: An experimental approach. *Management Science, 49*(4), 400–415.

Williams, D. (2006). On and off the'Net: Scales for social capital in an online era. *Journal of Computer-Mediated Communication, 11*(2), 593–628.

Part One

Theoretical Approaches to Cultural Proximity

1 Social Capital Theory and Its Application in Innovation Studies

A Theoretical Primer

Introduction

This chapter is intended to offer a theoretical contribution to the understanding of the concept of social capital and its effects on firm innovation through cultural proximity. Nowadays, the extensive distribution of knowledge and research revolutions has made it almost impossible for a single firm to have all the capabilities, resources, and knowledge required for innovation available within its own boundaries. The importance of firms' interaction and collaboration with other actors for the innovation process is underlined by several studies (Chesbrough, 2003; Freeman, 1991; Powell, Koput, & Smith-Doerr, 1996; Reidolf, 2016; Tether et al., 2002). Innovation is typically considered as the outcome of the joint efforts of different actors, including other firms, such as competitors and suppliers, and customers (von Hippel, 1988; Powell, 1990). These actors usually possess complementary resources, knowledge, and capabilities that the firm needs for its innovation process (Rosenberg, 1982).

Our conceptual framework is informed by the Resource Dependence Theory, which emphasizes how external forces affect the way firms manage those resources to compete in their environment (Pfeffer & Salancik, 1978). Resource Dependence Theory represents a unified theory of power at the organizational level of analysis (Casciaro & Piskorski, 2005) and predicts that a high degree of dependence in organizations is more likely to lead to the absorption of the sources of such dependence (Pfeffer, 1972; Pfeffer & Nowak, 1976; Pfeffer & Salancik, 1978). It provides an explanation not only of the reason why firms adopt innovation strategies, but also why such strategies may be contingent upon firms' environment. One broad tenet of particular relevance to our research is as follows: firms depend on other organizations controlling resources that are vital to them (Greening & Gray, 1994). Accordingly, firms make strategic choices regarding external relationships with the aim of "altering the system of constraints and dependencies confronting the organization" (Pfeffer & Salancik, 1978, p. 267). Drawing on this tenet, it is argued that the innovation strategies implemented by firms depend on the relationship-based strategies they adopt.

Within the context of the economic geography and innovation literature, scholars suggest that the persistent differences in firms' performance are partly determined by the resource endowments of the geographical area in which those firms are located. The importance of firm environment is supported by extensive empirical evidence with reference to the geographical concentration of innovative firms. If innovations were the mere result of public and codified knowledge, each firm should have the same probability of being innovative, and this probability should be independent of firm location. Therefore, the geographical distribution of innovations should be equivalent to the geographical distribution of firms. However, on an empirical level, these two distributions are shown to be substantially different: agglomerations of innovative activities are concentrated in particular geographical areas characterized by a process of entrance and the development of innovative firms. Silicon Valley in the USA is the best-known example of such concentration (Saxenian, 1994). Clearly, due to the differences in natural-resource endowments, such as infrastructures and investment in public and private knowledge production, regions have a great impact on the definition of firm innovation. However, while taking all these resources into account, we still lack a satisfactory explanation regarding some persistent differences between regions (Tappeiner, Hauser, & Walde, 2008). Social residue has long been regarded as a factor that might explain the differences in firm performance among regions, after considering other resource endowments (Perroux, 1950). These social factors are necessary to produce value from other sources, facilitating knowledge flows and, hence, leading to innovation.

In this chapter, we explore the role of social capital in promoting innovation by enhancing the benefit resulting from cultural proximity. While previous studies focus on the role of geographical proximity (Hauser, Tappenier, & Walde, 2007; Laursen, Masciarelli, & Prencipe, 2012; Laursen, Masciarelli, & Reichstein, 2016; Murphy, Huggins, & Thompson, 2016; Wang, Guidice, Zhou, & Wang, 2017), here, we focus on cultural proximity, suggesting that external social capital in the geographical area where the firm is located may play a role in determining firm innovation possibilities by increasing the benefit of cultural proximity. Culture is referred to as a set of attitudes, values, and beliefs in the minds of people and it arises from the socio-economic historical relationships of a group of people (Eklinder-Frick, Eriksson, & Hallén, 2014; Ouchi, 2004). It represents "the collective programming of the mind which distinguishes the members of one human group from another... the interactive aggregate of common characteristics that influences a human group's response to its environment" (Hofstede, 1980, p. 25).

Our main point is that the level of social capital developed in one environment -in the form of informal ties, social norms, and trust- may have a strong impact on cultural proximity, thereby influencing transaction models (Nahapiet & Ghoshal, 1998). Accordingly, the inventory of existing social relationships in society is then investigated (Piazza-Georgy, 2002) as a productive factor or, rather, as a tool that promotes the aggregation of productive factors, thus influencing various economic activities, such as innovation. In this chapter, social capital will be referred to as a public good that is accessible to all the subjects in a given territory.

This chapter is structured as follows: the first section provides an in-depth analysis of the concept of social capital along with an introduction to the possible instruments of measurement. The second section explores the competitive and complementary motivations behind an unequal territorial distribution of innovations, highlighting the reasons why it is legitimate to expect social capital to influence the territorial distribution of innovation. In the third section, a link between social capital, cultural proximity, and innovation is developed. The chapter concludes with a series of propositions aimed at describing the complex relationships regulating social capital, cultural proximity, and innovation.

Social Capital

The concept of social capital has drawn the attention of many researchers in various fields of study, such as political science (Putnam, Leonardi, & Nanetti 1993), sociology (Burt, 1992; Coleman, 1988; Lin, 1999), and economy (Beugelsdijk & van Schaik, 2005; Hauser et al., 2007; Knack & Keefer, 1997). Since the beginning of the 1990s, scholars have clarified their interest in the social dimensions shaping the economic performances of specific geographical contexts. In the field of economics, North (1990) stressed the importance of formal and informal institutions, that is, legal structures and normative rules of the game, in explaining existing differences in terms of economic performance. In political science, Putnam et al. (1993) showed that local civic associations laid the foundation for a widespread dissemination of knowledge and the development of social trust, thereby creating the conditions for effective governance and economic growth. In sociology, Evans (1995) discovered that whether a state was developmental or predatory, it was associated both to the capacity of its public institutions and to the nature of the relationship between state and society. These seminal works have inspired a pervasive and extensive literature on the role of social interaction and community participation merging around a general framework based on the idea of social capital (Woolcock & Narayan, 2000). Social capital entered the economic debate with the privilege of being an independent production factor (Woolcock & Narayan, 2000). The idea of social capital is that friends and associates constitute an important asset, and communities possessing a diverse and rich heritage of social ties and civic associations, will easily benefit from new opportunities (Isham, 2002). The classical economic literature identified three essential factors defining economic growth: land, labor, and physical capital. Schultz (1961) and Becker (1962) introduced the concept of human capital, arguing that the existence of trained and skilled workers is likely to affect economic growth. Economists have a clear view regarding the origins of social capital, as they see it as the product of iterated Prisoner's Dilemma games (Fukuyama, 1995). When the Prisoner's Dilemma is not repeated over time, defection produces a Nash equilibrium for both players and, therefore, the game does not result in co-operative outcomes. In repeated games, on the other hand, a tit-for-tat strategy involving co-operation for co-operation, and defection for defection, implies that both players will cooperate.

The term social capital was originally employed to capture the relational resources included in personal ties that are useful for personal development in social organizations (Jacobs, 1961; Loury, 1977). Bourdieu (Bourdieu, 1980) was the first to conceptualize social capital. He defined it as "the sum of the resources, actual or virtual, that accrue to an individual or group by virtue of possessing a durable network of more or less institutionalized relationships of mutual acquaintance and recognition" (Bourdieu, 1980, p. 2). According to Bourdieu (1980), social capital has two main components: (1) the social relation itself; social capital is a resource connected with social networks and group membership: "the volume of social capital possessed by a given agent depends on the size of the network of connections that he can effectively mobilize" (Bourdieu,

1986, p. 249); and (2) the quality shaped by the total amount of relationships between actors (Bourdieu, 1980). As regards the analysis of the concept of social capital, Bourdieu (1980) did not suggest any economic methodology; social capital is an attribute used to increase an agent's ability to advance his/her objectives. Coleman (1988) went one step further to conceptualize social capital, emphasizing the multidimensional nature of such a concept.

Social capital is defined by its function. It is not a single entity, but a variety of different entities, with two elements in common: they all consist in some aspect of social structures, and they facilitate certain actions of actors within the structure.

Social capital is related to some aspects of social structure that "make possible the achievement of certain ends that would not be attainable in absence" (Coleman, 1990, p. 302). Such a definition is relevant to the interpretation of the empirical evidence found in the social capital and embeddedness literature, and it represents a starting point for the measurement of social capital. By describing the wholesale diamond market in New York City, Coleman (1988) exemplified the influence of social capital on economic performance. The peculiarity of this market lies in the exchange, from one merchant to another, for the inspection of diamond bags worth hundreds of thousands of dollars. These exchanges take place without any formal insurance; therefore, there is no formal guarantee that the merchant receiving these diamond bags will return them. The social structure based on family, community, and religious ties, ensures that, in the event of failure to comply with the established economic obligations, the punishment will consist in the loss of these ties and the expulsion from the market. Social capital allows the market to work and transactions to be carried out; otherwise, it would be too expensive to establish insurance, and markets would not exist.

Putnam et al. (1993) provided the third main contribution to the conceptualization of social capital by looking at it as a community asset, and by defining social capital as the social structure that promotes coordination and cooperation. Putnam's idea of social capital refers to "connections among individuals, social networks and norms of reciprocity and trustworthiness that arise from them"(Putnam, 2000, p. 19). In his book Making Democracy Work, Putnam (1993) shows that, in Italy, the performance of regional governments is significantly related to the traditions of civic engagement, participation-level associations, voter turnout, and other manifestations of social capital. In his second publication, Bowling Alone: America's Declining Social Capital, Putnam (1995) claimed that, over the last decades, America had witnessed a massive decline in civic engagement, and that this decline was indicative of a decline in social connectedness among Americans. Putnam measured social capital in terms of voting turnout, attendance at public meetings, reported trust in government, and a significant decline in voluntary organizations membership.

Putnam's approach to social capital has influenced the most prominent analyses of social capital on a national (Knack & Keefer, 1997), regional (Hauser et al., 2007), and provincial level (Guiso, Sapienza, & Zingales, 2004). However, some scholars have criticized Putnam's approach. Among others, Portes and Landolt (1996) pointed out that Putnam's attention was only focused on the positive effects of social capital, without considering the negative ones. Portes (1998), in fact, suggested that a proper discussion of the negative aspects of social capital would avoid the mistake of deeming social capital as "unmixed blessings" and would also prevent social capital from becoming a "moralizing statement" (Portes, 1998, p. 15). The main doubts raised by Portes and Landolt (1996) and Portes (1998) can be summarized as follows: (i) insiders' accessibility to social capital may not always bring benefits for social welfare due to the exclusion of outsiders; (ii) it is crucial to specify the objectives for which individuals cooperate, since these objectives may be at odds with mainstream society (e.g. even criminal organizations embrace forms of cooperation); (iii) group obligations and participation may quench individual creativity, generating conformity among group members; in particular, the level of social control may represent a strong limitation to individual freedom as well as individual inventiveness and originality; (iv) the excessive demands of group members and the presence of social norms promoting mutual assistance may inhibit the entrepreneurial initiatives of community members.

It is therefore possible to conclude that social capital does not have an undisputed meaning nor a commonly accepted definition. The variety of definitions identified in the literature stems from the highly context-specific nature of social capital and the complexity of its conceptualization and operationalization. However, among the existing definitions, it is possible to find some degree of consensus that social capital should refer to networks of social interactions and the common point of the presented definitions of social capital is that they focus on social relations having productive benefits. In summary, from an examination of the suggested definitions, we can affirm that there are two main approaches to social capital; the first one considers social capital as the product of individual investment in the network of relationships (Coleman, 1988, 1990), while the second one considers social capital not as an individual product, but as the result of the interactions among people (Putnam, 1993, 1995). According to the first approach, social capital is produced individually through an individual investment in social relationships. According to the second one, social capital can be referred to as the institutions, relationships, and norms shaping the quality and quantity of social interactions within a society (Putman, 1993). "Social capital is not just the sum of the institutions that underpin a society, but it represents the glue that holds them together" (Dasgupta & Serageldin, 1999).

We therefore aim to analyze the effect of social capital on firm innovation. From the firms' perspective, social capital represents an external contingency that promotes cultural proximity by facilitating stable relationships, risk reduction, and fostering communication and cooperation among actors. Hence, social capital can be seen as a phenomenon that attempts to capture the complexity of the social structure in a given territory. The geographical dimension of social capital is explored by a wide range of studies (Beugelsdijk & van Schaik, 2005; Hauser et al., 2007; Knack & Keefer, 1997). The reason behind this choice lies in the idea that geography has a significant impact on social capital. Social relations are subject to distance costs since "the interdependences of different types of social relations make dense combinations of them dependent upon geographical proximity" (Lorenzen, 2007, p. 7). In defining the geographic boundaries of social capital, regions play a crucial role. Social capital originates from a collective process that may require many decades and may be deeply rooted in regional, institutional, historical, and cultural sediments that may be centuries old (Putnam, 1995). Therefore, social capital is a complex collective system of geographically bound social relations. However, social capital is a highly context-dependent phenomenon, and both the validity and reliability of a given measure of social capital depends on the level of aggregation considered. Social capital, however, is generated over time and is bounded in the cultural, traditional, and institutional setting of a given geographical area. In many countries, the boundaries of administrative regions have undergone a significant change over time.

The Empirics of Social Capital

Social capital is an intuitive and appealing concept; however, it is extremely difficult to measure. In fact, measurement problems emerge not only from the acknowledged scarcity of data but also from the complex and multidimensional nature of the concept itself. Not surprisingly, in view of the numerous disciplines approaching the concept of social capital, it is possible to measure social capital at different levels. Furthermore, social capital has multiple components that have a complex and different impact on the various outcomes. In other words, the specific components of social capital may be effective in explaining certain outcomes, but of little value in explaining others. Similarly, the various components of social capital may be important in explaining outcomes in some territories, but of limited importance, or even counterproductive, in others. The difficulties in identifying a unique, commonly accepted, conceptualization of social capital seem to drive the authors against the definition that better suits the outcomes and territories considered. Although various surveys are available, existing databases have been developed independently and often without an informed theoretical framework. As a result, the majority of the existing measures of social capital do not have a strong correlation with the theoretical definition. Often, imprecise items are employed (e.g. voting trends, trust in government, blond donation). Accordingly, contradictory results are commonly obtained since not all social capital measures will have the same relationship with the outcomes. Measurement difficulties are partially caused by definition problems. Data have been collected for different purposes and in heterogeneous contexts, and relate to different definitions of social capital.

Scholars are trying to establish an operational definition that identifies the key components of social capital. Social capital as a multidimensional concept is a commonly accepted idea. It includes different types of relationships and engagements; its components are numerous, varied, and in many instances, intangible (Dasgupta & Serageldin, 2000). Many of the existing studies on social capital employ data from the World Values Survey (Beugelsdijk & van Schaik, 2005; Hauser et al., 2007; Knack & Keefer, 1997). This research project consists of an investigation into social, cultural, and political, change carried out for representative national samples over 80 countries. This survey was developed through a study started by the European Values Survey group (EVS) in 1981. Four waves have been implemented since 1981, thus allowing a comparative analysis. The World Values Survey is of unquestionable value in cross-country studies on social capital. However, at a cross-country level, few data on firm performance are available. Firm-level surveys have a predominant national basis. Therefore, in order to evaluate the implications of social capital on firm performance, it becomes necessary to focus just on one country. Following Putnam's seminal study (1993), researchers dealing with the concept of social capital have started investigating its different aspects and declinations among Italian regions.

Social Capital and the Agglomeration of Innovation Activities

The continuous increase in technology license purchase and R&D process outsourcing arguably reflects the emergence of a more fine-grained inter-firm division of labor (Arora, Fosfuri, & Gambardella, 2001; Cassiman & Veugelers, 2006; Sobrero & Roberts, 2001). Whether the concentration of innovative activities is caused by the high costs of specific resource mobility, or is produced by spillovers that generate positive returns, a key role is in any case played by social capital. The idea that social capital may be a factor that favors the geographical concentration of innovation activities, arises from some evidence. The first point of evidence refers to information quality: informal and personal connections have proved to be better channels of information (Uzzi & Lancaster, 2003). This channel of knowledge exchange becomes even more important when knowledge is not merely exchanged, but is created during the innovation process, such as, for example, when product innovation produces process innovations in an industrial area. The second point of evidence refers to the ability of social capital to limit the opportunistic behaviors characterizing information and knowledge exchange. Stable relationships may represent an incentive for agents modifying their system of incentives, thus adding value to the social component of their action (Camerer & Knez, 1996). The public nature of knowledge often makes it difficult to define and establish property rights, which makes the role of social incentives for cooperation particularly important. The third point of evidence is that social capital fosters the relationships among agents that are stable and productive over time. Assuming that the value of innovation depends on many complementary investments, it is implied that a stable relationship path with other agents promotes high risk, although Pareto efficient, choices. In this regard, Pisano

(1990) discusses the case of firm cooperation in the R&D process. The complexity of R&D activities, as well as the risk associated with them, make the entire process difficult to define ex-ante. It follows that the contractual agreement cannot prevent opportunistic behaviors. In such cases, social capital, acting as an institutional mechanism to redress market failure, may support not only firm decision to cooperate in the R&D process, but also firm propensity to undertake riskier choices.

The value of innovation is often dependent on different and complementary investments. A history of stable and successful relationships induces individuals who coordinate their investment in complementary technologies to accept riskier but more remunerative solutions. Game theory analyzes these situations in stag hunt games (Skyrms, 2004). These games are characterized by multiple Nash equilibria, some of which prove to be riskier, although more remunerative for all players, while others appear safer, but less remunerative. When all players trust the other players, it is possible to reach the optimum equilibrium. On the contrary, when there is a high risk that some players will not trust the others, even the player inclined to trust will prefer a safer solution. When players successfully learn to trust each other, they tend to choose riskier, but more remunerative strategies. This phenomenon is known as analogical transfer, and it proves that trust can be learned and transferred from one situation to another. Therefore, trust becomes an asset that grows through the relationships between individuals and it can be usefully exploited in other fields. Stag hunt paradigm is employed to explain situations characterized by strategic or technological complementarities (Roberts, 2004).

Proposition Development

The research on social capital has considered a series of social behavior indicators, such as participation in social groups, associations and politics, weak and strong ties. By examining prior literature, it can be asserted that social capital is not only an important means of identification per se, but it is also a tool for managing different relationships in different contexts. This conceptualization implies that it is not necessarily critical to evaluate a particular social predisposition but, rather, the ability to manage a combination of relationships allowing the exchange of information and knowledge needed to produce innovation. This factor may be referred to as blending social capability of an individual. This capability is developed by means of strong interpersonal ties and identification with a social group.

Social capital is therefore vital for firm innovation since, through relationships, it fosters knowledge exchanges among actors involved in the innovation process. Knowledge originates from the application of the same interpretative schemes and mutual understanding; it derives from shared cultural traditions and habits, which stimulate the establishment of conventions and other institutional arrangements characterizing a cultural network (Bathelt, Malmberg, & Maskell, 2004; Eklinder-Frick & Åge, 2017). Thus, actors belonging to the same culture benefit from information, gossip, and news spread by just being there (Bathelt et al., 2004; Gertler 1995). Indeed, Howells and Bessant (2012) and Eklinder-Frick and Åge (2017) suggest that the social dimension of culture has been a continuous cross-fertilization field between researchers in management. Firms located in a geographical area having high levels of social capital are more likely to share the same set of norms, principles, and values which in turn produces benefit in terms of innovations.

This leaves us with the following propositions:

Proposition 1: The geographical features that favor innovations are difficult to move from one place to another. These features may be pre-existing or generated by firm activities, but their access is significantly influenced by cultural proximity.

In this regard, social capital represents a useful means to encourage the possibility of accessing the localized factors that create innovations.

Proposition 2: New knowledge is generated through information and knowledge exchange among many different communities.

These communities are characterized by different norms and rules. The norms and rules defining knowledge exchange are often the result of interpersonal relationships. Knowledge easily flows among people belonging to the same communities that refer to the same behavioral norms.

Proposition 3: The processes of creation and diffusion of innovation follow different paths. Some are essentially based on formal systems of relationship. In other cases, the exchange of knowledge and the creation of innovations cannot be controlled by means of formal procedures, but they imply trust, identification, and the respect of social norms.

These propositions lead to the following general statement:

> We should expect that social capital might have a different impact on different typologies of innovation depending on cultural proximity. Therefore, in order to analyze the effect of social capital on innovation, it is important to explore the role of cultural proximity.

Social capital is not claimed as a passe-partout useful to explain the agglomeration of innovation activities. In fact, we argue that social capital is far from being an absolute value but is, rather, a blending of various relational models. In particular, our aim is to highlight that social capital is a very complex concept, and that close attention should be paid to its assessment and to the variables employed to explain and define such a concept. Connecting social capital and cultural proximity might help to shed light on the role of social capital in promoting firm innovation in a given geographical area.

References

Arora, A., Fosfuri, A., & Gambardella, A. (2001). *Markets for technology: The economics of innovation and corporate strategy.* Cambridge, MA: The MIT Press.

Bathelt, H., Malmberg, A., & Maskell, P. (2004). Clusters and knowledge: Local buzz, global pipelines and the process of knowledge creation. *Progress in Human Geography, 28*(1), 31–56.

Becker, G. (1962). Investment in human capital: A theoretical analysis. *Journal of Political Economy, 70*(5), 9–49.

Beugelsdijk, S., & van Schaik, T. (2005). "Differences in social capital between 54 Western european regions. *Regional Studies, 39*(8), 1053–1064.

Bourdieu, P. (1980). Le capital social. Notes provisoires. *Actes, 31* (1), 2–3.

Bourdieu, P. (1986). The forms of capital. In J. Richardson (Ed.), *Handbook of theory and research for the sociology of education.* Westport, CT: Greenwood Press.

Burt, R. S. (1992). *Structural holes: The social structure of competition.* Cambridge, MA: Harvard University Press.

Camerer, O., & Knez, M. (1996). Coordination, organizational boundaries and fads in business practices. *Industrial and Corporate Change, 5*(1), 89–112.

Casciaro, T., & Piskorski, M. J. 2005. Power imbalance, mutual dependence, and constraint absorption: A closer look at resource dependence theory. *Administrative Science Quarterly, 50*(2), 167–199.

Cassiman, B., & Veugelers, R. (2006). In search of complementarity in innovation strategy: Internal R&D and external knowledge acquisition. *Management Science, 52*(1), 68.

Chesbrough, H. (2003). The era of open innovation. *Sloan Management Review, 44*, Summer, 35–41.

Coleman, J. (1988). Social capital in the creation of human capital. *American Journal of Sociology, 94*, 95–120.

Coleman, J. S. (1990). *Social capital*. Cambridge, MA: Harvard University Press.

Dasgupta, P., & Serageldin, I. (1999). *Social capital: A multifaceted perspective*. Washington, DC: The World Bank.

Dasgupta, P., & Serageldin, I. (2000). *Social capital: A multifaceted perspective*. Washington, DC: The World Bank.

Eklinder-Frick, J., & Åge, L. J. (2017). Perspectives on regional innovation policy–from new economic geography towards the IMP approach. *Industrial Marketing Management, 61*, 81–92.

Eklinder-Frick, J., Eriksson, L. T., & Hallén, L. (2014). Multidimensional social capital as a boost or a bar to innovativeness. *Industrial Marketing Management, 43*(3), 460–472.

Evans, P. (1995). *Embedded autonomy: States and industrial transformation*. Princeton, NJ: Princeton University Press.

Freeman, C. (1991). Networks of innovators: A synthesis of research issues. *Research Policy, 20*(5), 499–514.

Fukuyama, F. (1995). *Trust: The social virtues and the creation of prosperity*, pp. 264–268 in *World and I*. Vol. 10. USA: News World Communications, Inc.

Gertler, M. S. (1995). 'Being there': Proximity, organization, and culture in the development and adoption of advanced manufacturing technologies. *Economic Geography, 71*(1), 1–26.

Greening, D. W., & Gray, B. (1994). Testing a model of organizational response to social and political issues. *Academy of Management Journal, 37*(3), 467–498.

Guiso, L., Sapienza, P., & Zingales, L. (2004). The role of social capital in financial development. *American Economic Review, 94*(3), 526–556.

Hauser, C., Tappenier, G., & Walde, J. (2007). The learning region: The impact of social capital and weak ties on innovatio. *Regional Studies, 41*(1), 75–88.

von Hippel, E. (1988). *The sources of innovation*. New York: Oxford University Press.

Hofstede, G. (1980). *Culture's consequences: International differences in work-related values*. Vol. 5. Beverly Hills, CA: Sage Publications, Incorporated.

Howells, J., & Bessant, J. (2012). Introduction: Innovation and economic geography: A review and analysis. *Journal of Economic Geography, 12*(5), 929–942.

Isham, J. (2002). The effect of social capital on fertiliser adoption: Evidence from rural tanzania. *Journal of African Economies, 11*(1), 39–60.

Jacobs, J. (1961). *The death and life of great American cities*. New York: Random House.

Knack, S., & Keefer, P. (1997). Does social capital have an economic pay-off? A cross-country investigation. *Quarterly Journal of Economics, 112*(4), 1251–1288.

Laursen, K., Masciarelli, F., & Prencipe, A. (2012). Regions matter: How localized social capital affects innovation and external knowledge acquisition. *Organization Science, 23*(1), 177–193.

Laursen, K., Masciarelli, F., & Reichstein, T. (2016). A matter of location: The role of regional social capital in overcoming the liability of newness in R&D acquisition activities. *Regional Studies, 50*(9), 1537–1550.

Lin, N. (1999). Building a network theory of social capital. *Connections, 22*(1), 28–51.

Lorenzen, M. (2007). Social capital and localised learning: Proximity and place in technological and institutional dynamics. *Urban Studies, 44*(4), 799–817.

Loury, G. (1977). A dynamic theory of racial income differences. In P. A. Wallace & A. Mund (Eds.), *Women, minorities and employment discrimination* (pp. 153–186). Lexington, MA: Lexington Books.

Murphy, L., Huggins, R., & Thompson, P. (2016). Social capital and innovation: A comparative analysis of regional policies. *Environment and Planning C: Government and Policy, 34*(6), 1025–1057.

Nahapiet, J., & Ghoshal, S. (1998). Social capital, intellectual capital, and the organizational advantage. *Academy of Management Review, 23*(2), 242–266.

North, D. C. (1990). *Institutions, institutional change and economic performance.* Cambridge: Cambridge University Press.

Ouchi, W.G. (2004). The Z organization. In J. M. Shafritz, J. S. Ott, & Y. S. Jang, (Eds.), *Classics of organization theory sixth edition* (pp. 179–184). Boston: Wadsworth, Cengage Learning.

Perroux, F. (1950). Economic space: Theory and applications. *Quarterly Journal of Economics, 64*, 89–104.

Pfeffer, J. (1972). Size and composition of corporate boards of directors: The organization and its environment. *Administrative Science Quarterly, 17*, 218–228.

Pfeffer, J., & Nowak, P. (1976). Joint ventures and interorganizational interdependence. *Administrative Science Quarterly, 21*, 398–418.

Pfeffer, J., & Salancik, G. R. (1978). *The external control of organizations.* New York: Harper and Row.

Piazza-Georgy, B. (2002). The role of human and social capital in growth: Extending our understanding. *Cambridge Journal of Economics, 26*(4), 461–479.

Pisano, G. (1990). The R&D boundaries of the firm: An empirical analysis. *Administrative Science Quarterly, 35*(1), 153–176.

Portes, A. (1998). Social capital: Its origins and applications in modern sociology. *Annual Review of Sociology, 24*, 1–24.

Portes, A., & Landolt, P. (1996). The downside of social capital. *The American Prospect, 26*, 18–21.

Powell, W. (1990). Neither market nor hierarchy: Network forms of organization. *Research in Organizational Behaviour, 12*, 295–336.

Powell, W. W., Koput, K. W., & Smith-Doerr, L. (1996). Interorganizational collaboration and the locus of innovation: Networks of learning in biotechnology. *Administrative Science Quarterly, 41*, 116–145.

Putnam, R. D. (1993). The prosperous community: Social capital and public life. *The American Prospect, 13*(4), 35–42.

Putnam, R. D. (1995). Bowling alone: America's declining social capital. *Journal of Democracy, 6*(1), 65–78.

Putnam, R. D. (2000). *Bowling alone* (S. & Schuste, Ed.). New York.

Putnam, R. D., Leonardi, R., & Nanetti, R. Y. (1993). *Making democracy work*. Princeton, NJ: Princeton University Press.

Reidolf, M. (2016). Knowledge networks and the nature of knowledge relationships of innovative rural SMEs. *European Journal of Innovation Management, 19*(3), 317–336.

Roberts, J. M. (2004). What's 'social'about 'social capital'? *The British Journal of Politics and International Relations, 6*(4), 471–493.

Rosenberg, N. (1982). *Inside the black box*. New York: Cambridge University Press.

Saxenian, A. (1994). *Regional advantage: Culture and competition in silicon valley and route 128*. Cambridge, MA: Harvard University Press.

Schultz, T. W. (1961). Investment in human capital. *American Economic Review, 51*(1), 1–17.

Skyrms, B. (2004). *The stag hunt end the evolution of social structure*. Cambridge: Cambridge University Press.

Sobrero, M., & Roberts, E. (2001). The trade-off between efficiency and learning in interorganizational relationships for product development. *Management Science, 47*(4), 493–511.

Tappeiner, G., Hauser, C., & Walde, J. (2008). Regional knowledge spillovers: Fact or artifact? *Research Policy, 37*(5), 861–874.

Tether, B., Miles, I., Blind, K., Hipp, C., de Liso, N. & Cainelli, G. (2002). *Innovation in the service sector: Analysis of data collected under the community innovation survey (CIS-2)*. Manchester: Centre for Research on Innovation and Competition.

Uzzi, B., & Lancaster, R. (2003). Relational embeddedness and learning: The case of bank loan managers and their clients. *Management Science, 49*(4), 383–399.

Wang, S., Guidice, R., Zhou, Y., & Wang, Z. M. (2017). It's more complicated than we think: The implications of social capital on innovation. *Asia Pacific Journal of Management, 34*(3), 649–674.

Woolcock, M., & Narayan, D. (2000). Social capital: Implications for development theory, research, and policy. *The World Bank Research Observer, 15*(2), 225–249.

2 Cultural Dimensions, Social Axioms, and Cognitive Proximity

Introduction

Culture is referred to as a set of attitudes, values, and beliefs in the minds of people, and it derives from the socio-economic historical relationships of a group of people (Eklinder-Frick, Eriksson, & Hallén, 2014; Ouchi, 2004). It represents "the collective programming of the mind which distinguishes the members of one human group from another... the interactive aggregate of common characteristics that influences a human group's response to its environment" (Hofstede, 1980, p. 25).

Research on cultural values highlights the importance of cultural agreement among team members. From this perspective, incompatibilities in team members' and normative expectations can delay their ability to coordinate tasks, thus causing a negative relationship between cultural heterogeneity and firm performance (Denison & Mishra, 1995; Weber & Camerer, 2003). Specifically, cognitive proximity among team members increases the likelihood of collaborations by reducing the cognitive distance between individuals in search for mutual benefits (Lazega, 2009). As opposed to this point of view, the research performed by economic and cultural sociologists usually looks at cultural diversity as an advantage. In this conceptualization, heterogeneity is represented as a reflection of the cultural sharing available to individuals (Swidler, 1986). When organizational members have access to a broad array of cultural resources, the organization is assumed to have a bigger capacity for creativity and innovation (Feldman & Orlikowski, 2011; Friedland, 2012; Stark, Beunza, Girard & Lukács, 2011)

Team is conceived as a group of individuals who find themselves in a direct and immediate relationship, who exercise mutual influence, ultimately experiencing a sense of belonging that makes them feel part of it (Schaubroeck, Lam, & Peng, 2011). According to scholars, the performance of people who work in teams depends on a set of relational skills, including the ability of defining and pursuing goals that require cooperation, exchange of ideas, and collaboration. For this reason, the group should participate in a decision-making process that enables collaboration and exchange of knowledge, as well as an increase in the probability to achieve the goal through a unanimous decision. In fact, activities such as group discussion boost members' performance thus demonstrating that the most innovative and performing groups are those composed by individuals who actively participate in the decision-making process and face the dissent of the minority. The debate within a group, as well as being a way of sharing, can be a strategy to improve its performance.

A series of factors facilitating individual participation within a team have been identified. Social capital plays a prominent role: it creates the necessary conditions for the exchange and combination of knowledge; it gives access to network-based learning opportunities and it stimulates knowledge transfer (Inkpen & Tsang, 2005). Trust between individuals is also a crucial factor (Brinckmann & Hoegl, 2011). With the present chapter, we aim to show how sharing a similar view of the world on a personal issue, such as social axioms, can also affect the way a team performs.

The Operationalization of Cultural Values as Enablers of Proximity

Culture has emerged as a relevant aspect in management studies since the seminal, albeit controversial, contribution by Hofstede published in Organizational Dynamics in 1980. He claimed that there are no "general management theories" nor theories applicable to the world as a whole since cultural diversity makes theories emerging from the observation of local practice inapplicable. Following Hofstede's contribution, management scholars have started to pay attention to the role of culture in management.

In order to explore the importance of shared culture and value, it is crucial to define what is meant by culture and value in the present chapter. Following the definition of Parsons and Shils (1951), culture can be referred to as being "composed by a set of values, norms, and symbols that guide individual behaviour." Therefore, values appear to be among the main components of culture. As regards "values" we adopt the view of Rokeach (1973): "values are enduring beliefs that a specific mode of conduct or end state of existence is personally or socially preferable to an opposite or converse mode of conduct or end state of existence."

The first contributions focused on the diversity among nations, with particular emphasis on the collectivism/individualism dichotomy (Hofstede, 1980, 1993; House, Hanges, Javidan, Dorfman & Gupta, 2004; Kedia & Bhagat, 1988). In a collectivist society, individuals within a network or group see themselves primarily as parts of the whole. Conversely, when individualism prevails, individuals are motivated by personal interests and goals (Triandis, 1995). More specifically, Hofstede identified the following dimensions of culture that have an impact on cultural and economic behavior:

1   Collectivism/individualism: individualism is defined as "a loosely knit social framework in which people are supposed to take care of themselves and of their immediate families only," while collectivism "is characterized by a tight social framework in which people distinguish between in-groups and out-groups, they expect their in-group to look after them, and in exchange for that they feel they owe absolute loyalty to it" (Hofstede, 1980).

2   Power distance, "the extent to which a society accepts the fact that power in institutions and organizations is distributed unequally" (Hofstede, 1980).

3   Uncertainty avoidance, defined as

> the extent to which a society feels threatened by uncertain and ambiguous situations and tries to avoid these situations by providing greater career stability, establishing more formal rules, not tolerating deviant ideas and behaviours, and believing in absolute truths and the attainment of expertise.
>
> (Hofstede, 1980)

4   Masculinity/femininity, where masculinity is defined as "the extent to which the dominant values in society are 'masculine' – that is, assertiveness, the acquisition of money and things, and not caring for others, the quality of life, or people" (Hofstede, 1980), and femininity is configured as the opposite of masculinity.

5   Confucian dynamism (or long-term vs. short-term orientation) was developed later by Hofstede and Bond (1988). Long-term orientation refers to future-oriented values such as persistence and thrift, while short-term orientation refers to past- and present-oriented values such as respect for tradition and the fulfillment of social obligations.

Hofstede's contribution (1980) also has some limitations. First, Baskerville (2003) questions the possibility of studying culture by studying only national differences. In fact, a nation may be comprised of more than one cultural area (Goodenough, 1964; Wildavsky, 1989). The inquiry methodology represents another problem: observers are external (i.e. outside the culture) and this results in difficulties for the correct interpretation of processed data. Furthermore, Hofstede's approach is rather static. Cultural experiences change, but Hofstede, however, does not consider a dynamic approach (Scheuch, 1989). Despite these limitations, Hofstede's conceptualization and operationalization of cultural values (1980) paved the way for further studies. In fact, based on the assumption that Hofstede's classification is intended only for country-level studies, researchers have freely adapted it for individual-level studies. These adaptations provided a new way of considering, describing, and measuring culture (Bond, 2002). Strongly based on Hofstede's contribution, the GLOBE (Global Leadership and Organizational Behaviour Effectiveness) research program aimed at testing and extending Hofstede's previous findings. The GLOBE study was created by Robert House in 1991. At first, it was intended as an international research project on leadership. Later on, the study branched out into other aspects of national and organizational cultures. In the period 1994–1997, 170 voluntary collaborators collected data from about 17,000 managers in 951 organizations throughout the world. The GLOBE study is one of four major cross-cultural research projects carried out in the 1990s. Nine attributes of cultures, operationalized as quantitative dimensions, were investigated as major constructs in the GLOBE research program: (1) Uncertainty Avoidance, (2) Power Distance, (3) Collectivism I: Societal Emphasis on Collectivism, (4) Collectivism II: Family Collectivistic Practices, (5) Gender Egalitarianism, (6) Assertiveness, (7) Future Orientation, (8) Performance Orientation, and (9) Humane Orientation. These dimensions were selected on the basis of a review of the literature relevant to the measurement of culture in previous large-sample studies, and on the basis of existing cross-cultural theory.

Lastly, the contribution made by Hall and Hall (1989), who define culture through communication, will be briefly reviewed. They adopt behavioral-level dimensions to describe cultural differences. More specifically, culture is suggested to differ for the following three dimensions: various degrees of information coding through language (high/low context), different need for territorial space (high/low space), and changes in the use of time and working styles (monochronic/polychronic). The first dimension, context, refers to the degree used for information coding through language. In low context languages, most of the information is transferred as explicitly coded. In high context language, little information is explicit. The difference between these two approaches is the relevance attributed to context knowledge. The second dimension is "space." Individuals have, based on their cultural background, visible and invisible boundaries that must not be transgressed by others. This happens, for example, when others, in a normal conversation, do not maintain the usual distance and get too close. In such situations, individuals feel uncomfortable and offended. The last dimension identified is "time." Individuals can be divided into monochronic and polychronic. Monochronic individuals consider time as sequential, therefore they prefer to finish one task before they start a new one. Polychronic individuals, on the other hand, like to perform many tasks simultaneously. Unlike monochronic people, they do not feel disturbed if someone interrupts their work (Bouncken & Winkler, 2010; Hall & Hall, 1989; Winkler & Bouncken, 2011).

In this paragraph we provided a review of the most relevant approaches developed to operationalize cultural diversity, bearing in mind that cultural diversity in organizations can be put into operation with an almost infinite number of attributes which might potentially engender cultural diversity, for instance, religion (Hicks, 2002), skills, expertise, and experience (van der Vegt, Bunderson, & Oosterhof, 2006), as well as attitudes and personality (Harrison et al., 2002; Jehn, Chadwick, & Thatcher, 1997; Liao, Chuang, & Joshi, 2008). In the following paragraph, we will look into the work of Leung et al. (2002) that can be considered as an important starting point for understanding cultural proximity/diversity in teams.

Social Axioms, Cultural Proximity, and Team Performance

Leung et al. (2002) define social axioms as "generalized beliefs about oneself, the social and physical environment, or the spiritual world, [stated] in the form of an assertion about the relationship between two entities or concepts." In brief, according to Kwok Leung, they are nothing but a set of understandings summarized by how the world is completed. Social axioms are the premises that people build and on which they base the course of their lives in order to direct their actions and achieve their goals.

In this regard, the so-called Social Axioms Survey, which then led to the definition of a five-factor structure on general beliefs referred to social axioms, was conducted by Leung, mainly in Honk Kong and Venezuela, and afterward in the US, Germany, and Japan. Leung started with an examination of proverbs, cultural stories, interviews, and newspaper articles concerning the cultures of these countries and, grouping the results of this research, he obtained a pan-cultural analysis comprising 182 elements. Given the number of these factors, Leung then summarized them in an optimal structure consisting of 60 elements, or rather, given the English origin of the studies, items, which became part of the whole structure of the five social axiom dimensions.

The concept of social axiom intends to offer a cognitive interpretation of how individuals relate to others and to their environment as well as to examine the relevance of beliefs in different social contexts (Leung & Bond, 2004; Leung et al., 2002, 2005). Leung and Bond (2004) identify five dimensions of social axioms: social cynicism, reward for application, social complexity, fate control, and religiosity. They label and describe the five dimensions in the following terms:

1   Factor one is labeled *social cynicism* since its items represent a negative view of human nature, especially as it is easily corrupted by power, a biased view against some groups of people, a mistrust of social institutions, and a disregard of ethical means for achieving an end.

2   Factor two is labeled *social complexity* since its items suggest that there are no rigid rules, but rather multiple ways of achieving a given outcome, and that apparent inconsistency in human behavior is common.

3   Factor three is labeled *reward for application* since its items represent a general belief that effort, knowledge, careful planning, and the investment of other resources (Foa, 1971) will lead to positive results and help avoid negative outcomes.

4   Factor four is labeled *religiosity*, as its items assert the existence of supernatural forces and the beneficial functions of a religious belief.

5   Factor five is labeled *fate control*, as its items represent a belief that life events are predetermined and that people can in some way influence these outcomes. Interestingly, laypeople accept the logical contradiction between predetermination and their ability to alter predetermined events. Practices for avoiding bad luck are in fact commonplace in many cultures, and the contradiction existing in the simultaneous belief in both predetermination and possibilities for altering one's fate may be widespread in everyday life.

In the present work, we focus on the importance of sharing a common view in order to enhance team performance. To explore the effects of sharing common values on the possibility to improve knowledge sharing within a team, we developed a model that presents three mediators related to cultural proximity, that is, cultural compatibility, identity, and shared creativity norms. Compatibility, that is the congruence in organizational cultures among team members, influences the extent to which members are able to accomplish the synergistic potential (Madhok & Tallman, 1998). Social incompatibility may result in an inability to develop a harmonious relationship, thus negatively influencing collaborative effectiveness (Sarkar, Cavusgil, & Evirgen, 1997). Cultural compatibility represents the congruence in organizational philosophies, goals, and values. This dimension addresses broad issues related to team norms and value systems. We claim that in teams, cultural compatibility facilitates knowledge sharing and the development of a common language among team members (Sarkar, Echambadi, Cavusgil, & Aulakh, 2001). Based on this reasoning, we introduce the following proposition:

Proposition 1: In teams, high levels of cultural proximity in terms of cultural compatibility predict knowledge sharing among team members thereby positively influencing team performance.

Social identity theory postulates that individuals define themselves as members of more than one social group (e.g. profession, family, company) (Ashforth & Johnson, 2001; Meyer, Becker, & Van Dick, 2007; Tajfel & Turner, 2004). Here, we posit that identity has a positive effect on group performance by increasing trust towards other members and the willingness to share knowledge and information.

Proposition 2: In teams, high levels of cultural proximity in terms of identity predict knowledge sharing among team members thereby positively influencing team performance.

Shared creativity norms refer to expectations, interpretations, and meaning systems capturing shared language and codes among firms (Nahapiet & Ghoshal, 1998). These norms result from the behavior of organizations (both individually and collectively), they create cultural compatibility among partnering actors, and inform and govern knowledge sharing (Adler & Kwon, 2002). Shared creativity norms reflect shared beliefs, practices, and common ground characterizing the nature of cooperation among actors (Nahapiet & Ghoshal, 1998). Shared norms of creativity promote the establishment of cultural compatibility among team members, inform and shape cooperation, and lay the foundations for repeated interactions. Over time, these norms operate and represent an institutionalized set of rules that govern behavior without the need for formal contracts (Gulati, Nohria, & Zaheer, 2000). These rules produce a governance mechanism that enhances knowledge transfer. Kambil, Eselius, and Monteiro (2000) proposed that firms developing shared creativity norms with team members might catalyze their entrepreneurial abilities to generate higher knowledge sharing. Therefore, we expect that shared creativity norms will positively affect knowledge sharing within a team, thus increasing productivity.

Proposition 3: In teams, high levels of cultural proximity in terms of shared norms of creativity predict knowledge sharing among team members thereby positively influencing team performance.

References

Adler, P. S., & Kwon, S. W. (2002). Social capital: Prospects for a new concept. *The Academy of Management Review, 27*(1), 17–40.
Ashforth, B. E., & Johnson, S. A. (2001). Which hat to wear? The relative salience of multiple identities in organizational contexts. In M. A. Hogg & D. J. Terry (Eds.), *Social identity processes in organizational contexts* (pp. 31–48). Philadelphia: Psychology Press.
Baskerville, R. F. (2003). Hofstede never studied culture. *Accounting, Organizations and Society, 28*(1), 1–14.
Bond, M. H. (2002). Reclaiming the individual from hofstede's ecological analysis--a 20-year odyssey: Comment on Oyserman et al.(2002). *Psychological Bulletin, 128*, 73–77.
Bouncken, R. B., & Winkler, V. A. (2010). National and cultural diversity in transnational innovation teams. *Technology Analysis & Strategic Management, 22*(2), 133–151.
Brinckmann, J., & Hoegl, M. (2011). Effects of initial teamwork capability and initial relational capability on the development of new technology-based firms. *Strategic Entrepreneurship Journal, 5*(1), 37–57.
Denison, D. R., & Mishra, A. K. (1995). Toward a theory of organizational culture and effectiveness. *Organization Science, 6*, 204–223.
Eklinder-Frick, J., Eriksson, L. T., & Hallén, L. (2014). Multidimensional social capital as a boost or a bar to innovativeness. *Industrial Marketing Management, 43*(3), 460–472.
Feldman, M. S., & Orlikowski, W. J. (2011). Theorizing practice and practicing theory. *Organization Science, 22*, 1240–1253.

Foa, U. G. (1971). Interpersonal and economic resources. *Science, 171*(3969), 345–351.

Friedland, R. (2012). The institutional logics perspective: A new approach to culture, structure, and process. *M@n@gement, 15*(5), 583.

Goodenough, W. H. (1964). *Explorations in cultural anthropology. Essays in honour of George Peter Murdock.* New York: McGraw-Hill.

Gulati, R., Nohria, N., & Zaheer, A. (2000). Guest editors' introduction to the special issue: strategic networks. *Strategic Management Journal, 21*(3), 199–201.

Hall, E. T., & Hall, M. R. (1989). *Understanding cultural differences.* Garden City, NY: Intercultural Press.

Harrison, D. A., Price, K. H., Gavin, J. H., & Florey, A. T. (2002). Time, teams, and task performance: Changing effects of surface- and deep-level diversity on group functioning. *Academy of Management Journal, 45*(5), 1029–1045.

Hicks, D. A. (2002). Spiritual and religious diversity in the workplace: Implications for leadership. *The Leadership Quarterly, 13*(4), 379–396.

Hofstede, G. (1980). *Culture's consequences: International differences in work-related values.* Vol. 5. Beverly Hills, CA: Sage Publications, Incorporated.

Hofstede, G. (1993). Cultural constraints in management theories. *The Academy of Management Executive, 7*(1), 81–94.

Hofstede, G., & Bond, M. H. (1988). The confucius connection: From cultural roots to economic growth. *Organizational Dynamics, 16*(4), 5–21.

House, R. J., Hanges, P. J., Javidan, M., Dorfman, P. W., & Gupta, V. (2004). *Culture, leadership, and organizations: The GLOBE study of 62 societies.* Thousand Oaks, CA: Sage Publications.

Inkpen, A. C., & Tsang, E. W. K. (2005). Social capital, networks, and knowledge transfer. *Academy of Management Review, 30*(1), 146–165.

Jehn, K., Chadwick, C., & Thatcher, S. (1997). To agree or not to agree: The effects of value congruence, individual demographic dissimilarity, and conflict on workgroup outcomes. *International Journal of Conflict Management, 8*(4), 287–305.

Kambil, A., Eselius, E. D., & Monteiro, K. A. (2000). Fast venturing: The quick way to start web businesses. *Sloan Management Review, 41*(4), 55–68.

Kedia, B. L., & Bhagat, R. S. (1988). Cultural constraints on transfer of technology across nations: Implications for research in international and comparative management. *Academy of Management Review, 13*(4), 559–571.

Lazega, E. (2009). Cooperation among competitors. Its social mechanisms through network analyses. *Sociologica, 3*(1), 0.

Leung, K., Bhagat, R. S., Buchan, N. R., Erez, M., & Gibson, C. B. (2005). Culture and international business: Recent advances and their implications for future research. *Journal of International Business Studies, 36*(4), 357–378.

Leung, K., & Bond, M. H. (2004). Social axioms: A model for social beliefs in multicultural perspective. In M. P. Zanna (Ed.), *Advances in experimental social psychology*, (Vol. 36, pp. 119–197). Cambridge, Massachusetts: Elsevier Academic Press.

Leung, K., Bond, M. H., de Carrasquel, S. R., Muñoz, C., Hernández, M., Murakami, F., ... & Singelis, T. M. (2002). Social axioms: The search for universal dimensions of general beliefs about how the world functions. *Journal of Cross- Cultural Psychology. Journal of Cross-Cultural Psychology, 33*, 286–302.

Liao, H., Chuang, A., & Joshi, A. (2008). Perceived deep-level dissimilarity: Personality antecedents and impact on overall job attitude, helping, work withdrawal, and turnover. *Organizational Behavior and Human Decision Processes, 106*(2), 106–124.

Madhok, A., & Tallman, S. B. (1998). Resources, transactions and rents: Managing value through interfirm collaborative relationships. *Organization Science, 9*(3), 326–339.

Meyer, J., Becker, T. E., & Van Dick, R. 2007. Social identities and commitments at work: toward an integrative model. *Human Resources Abstracts, 42*, 665.

Nahapiet, J., & Ghoshal, S. (1998). Social capital, intellectual capital, and the organizational advantage. *Academy of Management Review, 23*(2), 242–266.

Ouchi, W.G. (2004). The Z organization. In J. M. Shafritz, J. S. Ott, & Y. S. Jang, (Eds.), *Classics of organization theory sixth edition* (pp. 179–184). Boston: Wadsworth, Cengage Learning.

Parsons, T. and Shils, E. A. (1951). Values, motives, and systems of action. In T. Parsons and E. A. Shils (eds.), *Toward a general theory of action* (pp. 47–275). Cambridge, MA: Harvard University Press.

Rokeach, M. (1973). *The nature of human values.* Vol. 438. New York: Free Press.

Sarkar, M. B., Echambadi, R., Cavusgil, S. T., & Aulakh, P. S. (2001). The influence of complementarity, compatibility, and relationship capital on alliance performance. *Journal of the Academy of Marketing Science, 29*(4), 358–373.

Sarkar, M., Cavusgil, S. T., & Evirgen, C. (1997). A commitment-trust mediated framework of international collaborative venture performance. *Cooperative Strategies: North American Perspectives, 1*, 255–285.

Schaubroeck, J., Lam, S. S. K., & Peng, A. C. (2011). Cognition-based and affect-based trust as mediators of leader behavior influences on team performance. *Journal of Applied Psychology, 96*(4), 863.

Scheuch, E. K. (1989). Theoretical implications of comparative survey research: Why the wheel of cross-cultural methodology keeps on being reinvented. *International Sociology, 4*(2), 147–167.

Stark, D., Beunza, D., Girard, M., & Lukács, J. (2011). *The sense of dissonance: Accounts of worth in economic life.* Oxford: Princeton University Press.

Swidler, Ann. (1986). Culture in action: Symbols and strategies. *American Sociological Review, 51*(2), 273–286.

Tajfel, H., & Turner, J. C. (2004). The Social Identity Theory of Intergroup Behavior. In J. T. Jost & J. Sidanius (Eds.), *Key readings in social psychology. Political psychology: Key readings* (pp. 276–293). East Sussex, United Kingdom: Psychology Press.

Triandis, H. C. (1995). *Individualism & collectivism.* Boulder, CO: Westview Press.

van der Vegt, G. S., Bunderson, J. S., & Oosterhof, A. (2006). Expertness diversity and interpersonal helping in teams: Why those who need the most help end up getting the least. *Academy of Management Journal, 49*(5), 877–893.

Weber, R. A., & Camerer, C. F. (2003). Cultural conflict and merger failure: An experimental approach. *Management Science, 49*(4), 400–415.

Wildavsky, A. (1989). Frames of reference come from cultures: A predictive theory. In M. Freilich (Ed.), *The relevance of culture* (pp. 58–74). New York: Bergin & Garvey.

Winkler, V. A., & Bouncken, R. B. (2011). How does cultural diversity in global innovation teams affect the innovation process? *Engineering Management Journal, 23*(4), 24–35.

3 Entrepreneurship and Cultural Proximity

Introduction

In this chapter, we will refer to the literature on entrepreneurship (Shane, Venkataraman, & MacMillan, 1995; Venkataraman, 1997) and to the upper echelons theory (Hambrick & Mason, 1984) to conceptualize the relationship between the characteristics and experience of entrepreneurs and the effects that cultural proximity has on new ventures. First, the key theoretical constructs used in this chapter will be outlined, then our research propositions will be presented. The present research considers the literature on entrepreneurship involving the discovery, definition, and exploitation of new entrepreneurial opportunities (Shane & Venkataraman, 2000), including the identification of new problems and solutions, the imagination of novel possibilities, the vision of situations from different perspectives, and the collection of information from various sources (Geroski, 2000).

Based on the upper echelons theory, we explain whether and how entrepreneurs benefit from cultural proximity in the innovative process. The upper echelons theory has shown that entrepreneurs are responsible for the decisions to initiate strategic changes (Child, 1972; Hambrick, 1984) and that the skills, knowledge, and background of the founding team may have a key role in the determination of major strategic changes (Finkelstein & Hambrick, 1990; Wiersema & Bantel, 1992). According to this theory, organizational outcome, strategic choice, and performance levels are influenced by the experience and personal characteristics of the entrepreneur (Hambrick & Mason, 1984). This theory is built on the assumption that individuals have a bounded rationality, which hinders their capability to access, process, and use information (Hambrick, 1984). Hambrick and Mason (1984) state that, due to such difficulties, the cognitive basis of individuals is likely to affect their ability to discern (i.e. observe and distinguish the differences), perceive (i.e. know reality through the elaboration of external stimuli), and interpret (i.e. give meaning through knowledge).

The first studies on the upper echelons theory mainly focused on the composition, characteristics, and behavior of top management teams; in recent years, however, greater attention has been paid to the way personality traits of entrepreneurs and their behavior affect strategic and organizational performance (Abatecola, 2013). The most frequently investigated strategic and organizational outcomes are diversification, innovation, international alliances, and risk propensity or aversion (Abatecola, 2013; Carpenter, Geletkanycz, & Sanders, 2004; Finkelstein & Hambrick, 1990; Hambrick, 2007). While recognizing the critical role of entrepreneurs in determining the strategic change of firms, prior research has paid attention to the specific case of entrepreneurs in technology-based firms. As a result, little is known about the effects of entrepreneurs' past experiences on the strategic decisions taken by these firms. As opposed to the traditional literature on entrepreneurship, which tends to attribute the success and failure of technology-based firms to single individuals (Gartner, 1988), this chapter stresses that these firms are generally launched and managed by a team of entrepreneurs. Therefore, the purpose of the present chapter is to shed further light on the role of founders in defining the strategic change of technology-based firms.

Specifically, this chapter will discuss: (1) whether, how, and why the characteristics of the entrepreneur accelerate the innovation of technology-based firms, and (2) whether and how social capital promotes the development of technology-based firms through cultural proximity.

As regards the first area of investigation, previous upper-echelon research reported that while some entrepreneurs show a clear propensity for change that fosters innovation, others exhibit a status quo. The basic factor that allows some entrepreneurs to be more open about change than others lies in their past experiences. This supports team heterogeneity in the team of founders. In this respect, Webber and Donahue (2001) suggest to distinguish the dimensions of heterogeneity that are directly related to the job from those dimensions that are not job-related. Job-related factors are defined by previous distinct work experiences of the entrepreneurs (Pelled, 1996; Simons, Pelled, & Smith, 1999). In high technology-based ventures, the background of entrepreneurs may be more important than other factors – e.g. age and gender - since the former characteristic may be a more important asset to access new resources and knowledge which represent the essential advantage of heterogeneity in complex industries (e.g. Carpenter, 2002; Keck, 1997). This heterogeneity, in fact, is likely to provide the team of entrepreneurs with a greater range of knowledge sources than would otherwise be accessible to teams whose members share similar/ common prior experiences. Furthermore, team heterogeneity is expected to be beneficial for strategic change, as differences between team members may stimulate debates questioning the appropriateness of an existing strategy and allow them to develop a wider range of strategic alternatives, and to better assess the feasibility of those alternatives. First, heterogeneity provides the team of founders of a high-technology venture with a broader spectrum of professional perspectives.

This variety of perspectives is considered to be advantageous in management processes that imply creative thinking such as those involving strategic change (Milliken & Martins, 1996). Additionally, as mentioned above, team heterogeneity broadens the range of accessible knowledge sources (Keck, 1997; Knight et al., 1999; Pitcher & Smith, 2001). This is also in accordance with the social capital theory discussed in Chapter 1. The perspective adopted in this project includes a social view of the individual, exploring the role of social capital. The term social capital was originally introduced to illustrate the relational resources, rooted in personal ties, that are developed by individuals in the social organization of a community (Jacobs, 1961). Social capital has been found to provide learning opportunities (Powell, Koput, & Smith-Doerr, 1996); facilitate knowledge sharing; increase legitimacy (Higgins & Gulati, 2003), norms observance, and social control (Coleman, 1990b); and facilitate joint problem-solving arrangements (Burt, 1992). Past work experiences define the social capital possessed by the founders' team as well as the possibility to access external sources of knowledge.

With regard to the second question, we assume that social capital which is geographically bound and connected to the firm environment may provide easier access to external sources of knowledge through cultural proximity. Geographically bound social capital is a collective good integrated into the environment of firms (Knack & Keefer, 1997; Putnam, 1993). Putnam (1993) introduced this approach to social capital by recognizing that regional associations and informal ties lay the foundations for knowledge sharing and complementarities, accelerate problem recognition, promote resource accessibility, and reduce the time for monitoring partners, thus creating the conditions for a successful development. Based on this approach, social capital is a geographically bound phenomenon representing a central external contingency for firms: critical resources often expand beyond firm boundaries and are integrated into an external context. Therefore, social environment is an important source for new ideas and geographically bound social capital is a necessary mechanism to produce value from other sources, facilitating the dissemination of information and, hence, leading to competitive advantage. Knowledge spreading through imitation and active knowledge sharing within the same geographical context is a concept highlighted by several authors (Rosenthal & Strange, 2003). The existence of these effects is based on the idea that a short geographical distance brings organizations together, fosters interactions that are rich in information, and facilitates the exchange, particularly of tacit knowledge between the actors (Gilly & Torre, 2000). As the distance between the actors increases, so does the difficulty of transferring tacit forms of knowledge as well as codified knowledge, since its interpretation and use require tacit knowledge, and, therefore, spatial proximity (Howells, 2002). Geographical proximity is particularly relevant for industries where knowledge is "person-embodied, concept-dependent, spatially sticky, and socially accessible only through direct physical interaction" (Morgan, 2004, p. 12).

Geographically bound social capital may be advantageous for new technology-based ventures. During the first years in the life of a firm, geographically bound social capital may define the interplay between technology-based ventures and established firms and institutions (i.e. competitors, clients, suppliers, universities). We pose that geographically bound social capital, by increasing the level of cultural proximity, can enhance the growth of new technology-based ventures. In sum, the present research aims to explore the following propositions:

Proposition 1: New technology-based ventures' proposition: There will be a positive relationship between the heterogeneity of the founders' team and firm openness to change.

Proposition 2: Co-founders' social capital - technology-based firms' proposition: high levels of founders' social capital -both internal and external social capital- accelerate the innovation process in technology-based firms through cultural proximity.

Theoretical Background

Entrepreneurs belonging to networks are shown to have a greater ability to promote innovation in their firms (Padgett & Powell, 2011). Knowledge is not only cognitive and abstract but also contextual, generated through a learning process in both organized and accidental meetings between actors. The literature on social capital provides a theoretical framework to explain the effect of social relationships on the innovation process (Adler & Kwon, 2002; Mu, Peng, & Love, 2008; Pérez-Luño, Medina, Lavado, & Rodríguez, 2011; Tidd, 1995). Social capital has been perceived as the missing link that goes beyond the traditional forms of economic capital and provides a connection between social relationships and the creation of knowledge (Eklinder-Frick & Åge, 2017). Knowledge also results from the application of the same interpretative schemes and mutual understanding; it originates from shared cultural traditions and habits, which encourage the establishment of conventions and other institutional arrangements that characterize a cultural network (Bathelt, Malmberg, & Maskell, 2004; Eklinder-Frick & Åge, 2017). Therefore, cultural proximity helps actors to benefit from the dissemination of information, gossip, and news by just being there (Bathelt et al., 2004; Iturrioz, Aragón, & Narvaiza, 2015). Molina-Morales, García-Villaverde, and Parra-Requena (2014) suggest that cultural homogeneity represents a measure of the extent to which actors perceive, interpret, understand, and evaluate the world in a similar way. As regards firms, prior literature provides contradictory findings related to the role of cultural homogeneity on firm performance. Some findings show that it fosters knowledge exchange between organizations (Knoben & Oerlemans, 2006), boosts innovation (Dakhli & De Clercq, 2004) as well as organizational performance (Krause, Handfield, & Tyler, 2007), and limits conflicts and misunderstandings related to communication issues (Inkpen & Tsang, 2005). This similarity increases the likelihood of inter-organizational collaborations by reducing the cognitive distance between partnering organizations searching for mutual benefits, and it provides an identity for organizations looking for exchange partners (Lazega, 2009). On the other hand, the literature on the formation of alliances argues that organizations will be inclined to create collaborative ties in order to access specialized complementary assets (Colombo, Delmastro, & Rabbiosi, 2007), and that technological competencies, absorptive capacity, and the cognitive distance between organizations are vital (Inkpen & Tsang, 2005; Nooteboom, 1994; Wuyts, Colombo, Dutta, & Nooteboom, 2005).

Social capital (Portes, 1998) has both advantages and disadvantages for the firms involved. The rationale is that the value of a particular network depends on what the firm wants to achieve from this membership (Adler & Kwon, 2002). The distinction between bridging and bonding social capital in cultural networks is both important and useful in the context of promoting innovation. Putnam (2000) notes that while bonding social capital requires strong connections within a group, bridging social capital involves interactions between different social groups and looser bonds between the actors (Eklinder-Frick, Eriksson, & Hallén, 2012, 2014). Strong ties are crucial in bonding social capital: tie strength, in fact, increases the willingness and ability of the contacts in the entrepreneur's network to provide the required resources (Batjargal, 2003; Coleman, 1990a). From an analysis of the advantages of bonding social capital the presence of strong ties increases the determination and ability of the entrepreneur to establish closer relationships with other network members that will grant access to valuable resources and knowledge (Batjargal, 2003; Ceci, Masciarelli, & Poledrini, 2019; Sajuria, vanHeerde-Hudson, Hudson, Dasandi, & Theocharis, 2015). In this case, relational trust and benefits, such as decreased transaction costs between strong ties (Dasgupta & Serageldin, 2000), prove to be important. In circumstances of serious asymmetry of information, such as the development of innovation, social capital can be beneficial since it can represent an indirect form of social control to regulate opportunistic or antisocial behaviors (Coleman, 1990b; Masciarelli, 2011). Bonding social capital facilitates the dissemination of information and, specifically, private information. Individuals involved in the same cultural network know how others behave in relation to consumption or savings; they can tell how much others work for the sake of society and how and whether they respect social and individual rules. The information collected is both private and meaningful and it provides the information collector with sufficient knowledge to identify reliable or unreliable individuals (Eklinder-Frick et al., 2014).

Bonding social capital implies that actors behaving in antisocial or opportunistic ways within a network would lose their reputation and, eventually, be excluded from the social system since their behavior has become known to all the members of the network. Despite the benefits described above, bonding social capital can have some drawbacks as well. It has been suggested by Hoyman and

Faricy (2009) that strong bonds between actors in homogeneous groups can hinder innovation by increasing complacency and isolating internal actors from external ones. This insight is based on the homophily theory, which posits the formation of strong overlapping ties between socially proximate individuals, thus making the links with people from distant social circles more likely to be weak (McPherson, Smith-Lovin, & Cook, 2001). Therefore, the risk of lock-in (Gargiulo & Benassi, 2000; Grabher, 1993; Uzzi, 1997) and cultural over-embeddedness (Granovetter, 1985; Laursen, Masciarelli, & Prencipe, 2012; Uzzi, 1997) that can follow the bonding dimension of social capital should not be overlooked (Eklinder-Frick et al., 2012; Soetanto, Huang, & Jack, 2018).

Bridging social capital stresses the strategic role of weak ties (Granovetter, 1973) and structural holes (Burt, 1992). According to Granovetter (Granovetter, 1973), firms can access a greater amount of new information through temporary or intermittent connections, and cohesive networks do not offer the most favorable environment for innovation. Granovetter (1973) makes use of the term 'bridging' to indicate how weak ties create bridges between actors in a social context. Weak ties make communication easier, thus generating advantageous flows of information and resources among different groups (Granovetter, 1973, 1983). In his theory on structural holes, Burt (Burt, 1992) defined them as the absence of direct relationships among the network contacts of the focal actor, suggesting that firms benefit from timely access to and control over external resources through ties with others actors that are not directly connected (Batjargal, 2010; Burt, 1992).

Florida (2002) connects bridging social capital with what he refers to as the creative class, and relates innovation to loose bonds between different social groups, contributing to an open and innovative society. Patulny and Svendsen (2007) portray the consequences of close bonding as widespread distrust, prejudice, nepotism, lack of cooperation, group isolation, social poverty, and neighborhood conflicts. Since bridging social capital is based on a lower level of trust between actors compared to bonding social capital (Ahuja, 2000), the information shared among collaborating firms often proves to be irrelevant to the innovation process. Firms share critical information with trusted and familiar actors gained through bonding social capital (Gabbay & Zuckerman, 1998). The presence of both bridging and bonding social capital makes it possible to simultaneously capture the dynamics of both openness and closure within small exclusive groups (Leonard, 2004). Bridging and bonding social capital are not mutually exclusive and the right combination of the two is the optimal policy recommendation (Leonard, 2004; Svendsen & Svendsen, 2004).

Team of Founders' Heterogeneity and Innovation

A small business is an extension of the entrepreneur (Gatewood, Shaver, & Gartner, 1995; Gilbert, 2006). The upper echelons theory shows the reason why entrepreneur personality influences the strategic choices and, therefore, the performance of his or her business (Hambrick & Mason, 1984). Scholars have focused mainly on the relationship between entrepreneur personality and innovation in established firms (Baron & Markman, 2003; Kato, Okamuro, & Honjo, 2015; King, Walker, & Broyles, 1996; Patterson, 1999, 2002). In particular, King et al. (1996) reveal a stable set of personality features that consistently connect innovation and creativity.

Every person is characterized by both observable and unobservable traits (Brody, 2013). Observable traits are those that can be easily verified such as age, gender, levels of education, socioeconomic background, and financial position (Hambrick & Mason, 1984), while unobservable ones are personality traits that shape the individual's behavior (Plummer, 2000). Personality traits are individual characteristics that describe why individuals behave differently in similar situations (Leonelli, Ceci, & Masciarelli, 2016, 2019; Nga & Shamuganathan, 2010). Prior studies have focused on the observable characteristics of entrepreneurs and their effects on strategy and firm performance (Boone, De Brabander, & Van Witteloostuijn, 1996). More recently, scholars have also addressed the role of entrepreneur personality traits in the management of new ventures (O'Reilly, Caldwell, Chatman, & Doerr, 2014).

The personality traits of entrepreneurs have a strong influence on business decisions especially in small and young firms (Kickul & Gundry, 2002; Lee, Tsang, & Littunen, 2001; Littunen, 2000): in order to successfully manage new business ventures, entrepreneurs should be innovative and risk-takers, they should be able to recognize and take advantage from opportunities, while being able to make quick decisions under uncertainty and resource-limited conditions (Ardichvili, Cardozo, & Ray, 2003; Baum, Frese, & Baron, 2014; Baum & Locke, 2004; Kickul & Walters, 2002; Rauch & Frese, 2007). Several studies have explored the relationship between entrepreneurial traits and firm performance. Some have considered entrepreneurial orientation and risk-taking behavior (Haroon Hafeez,

Shariff, Noor, & Mad Lazim, 2012; Leonelli, Masciarelli, & Fontana, 2019; Zhao, Seibert, & Lumpkin, 2010), others have looked deeper into entrepreneur narcissism (Chatterjee & Hambrick, 2007; Leonelli et al., 2016; Wales, Patel, & Lumpkin, 2013), others have focused on the Big Five traits (i.e. openness to experience, conscientiousness, extraversion, agreeableness, and neuroticism).

Recently, literature has focused on the role of narcissism (Leonelli & Masciarelli, 2019): entrepreneur narcissism. Narcissistic people easily emerge as leaders in groups and are quickly perceived by others as real leaders in entrepreneurial firms (Engelen, Neumann, & Schmidt, 2016; Judge, LePine, & Rich, 2006). Narcissism only began to be considered as a personality trait at the end of the twentieth century, while earlier, it had been considered as a psychological disorder or pathology (see Freud, 2014). Narcissist is seen as arrogant, haughty, grandiose, overbearing, and authoritarian and as someone who deserves special treatment, requires admiration, ignores other people's feelings, lacks empathy, and overestimates his abilities (Campbell, Goodie, & Foster, 2004; Chatterjee & Hambrick, 2007; Rosenthal & Pittinsky, 2006; Wales et al., 2013). In brief, narcissism encompasses a wide array of entirely negative characteristics, a synonym for every self-absorbed and self-centered behavior (Maccoby, 2003). In the literature, many scholars show that narcissism is sometimes confused with other important personality traits; specifically with self-esteem (Chatterjee & Hambrick, 2007), core self-evaluation (Simsek, Heavey, & Veiga, 2010), overconfidence (Bollaert & Petit, 2010), and hubris (Petit & Bollaert, 2012).

Here, team heterogeneity, referred to entrepreneurial team's personality in new technology-based ventures, is assumed to provide firms with a larger spectrum of perspectives which might be conducive to innovation.

Proposition 1: In new technology-based ventures, founders' heterogeneity in terms of personality traits promotes the development of the innovation process.

The perspective adopted in this chapter includes a social vision of individual. Here, the need for a deeper investigation of the social capital in the founders' team is suggested since the latter plays an essential role in shaping the behavior of technology-based firms. The social capital of the founders' team can be divided into internal social capital and external social capital. Internal social capital increases the proximity that exists between co-founders (e.g. former joint work experiences; shared norms and experiences), while external social capital, that concerns the extent to which each founder is rooted in the context where the firm operates (e.g. number of years the co-founder lived in the firm's region) is likely to increase heterogeneity.

We assume that internal and external social capital have a different effect based on the innovation stage. Current research posits that the innovation process can be divided into two main stages: opportunity recognition and innovation implementation (Maine, Soh, & Dos Santos, 2015; Perry-Smith & Mannucci, 2017; Rogers, 2010). Opportunity recognition is the first stage in the innovation process and it includes the possibility to identify a new and profitable business, product, or service (Barringer & Ireland, 2010). It is about looking at situations from different perspectives (Geroski, 2000; West & Bogers, 2014). It refers to the identification of a market need by means of the creative combination of resources in order to provide a higher added value (Ardichvili et al., 2003). Opportunities may arise, for example, as the consequence of changes in the industry or technology or unexpected events in a particular market (Drucker, 2002). In this chapter, we agree with the vision of the discovery of business opportunities that suggest that these opportunities arise from information asymmetries with respect to the real value of resources and the resulting value of the combination of those resources in output (Sarasvathy, Dew, Velamuri, & Venkataraman, 2003). The implementation stage in the innovation process refers to the application of already created ideas and involves the transformation of the new idea into a product or process innovation. Therefore, innovation implementation involves development (adaptation of scientific knowledge to meet the potential demand of the customer or user), commercialization (production phase leading to the distribution of the new product or service) and diffusion/adoption (spreading of the innovation to potential adopters) (Rogers, 2010). It implies the translation of ideas through their development and commercialization, and the diffusion of the resulting innovation among potential adopters (Basadur & Gelade, 2006).

External social capital is a form of bridging social capital emphasizing the strategic role of weak ties that create bridges between actors in a social context (Granovetter, 1973). Weak ties make communication easier and, therefore, results in the generation of beneficial flows of information and resources between different groups (Granovetter, 1973, 1983). External social capital enhances heterogeneity and grants access to different knowledge sources. Internal social capital represents a form of bounding social capital that creates strong ties within the founders' team: tie strength increases the determination and ability of actors to provide the required resources (Batjargal, 2003; Coleman, 1990b). In circumstances of serious information asymmetry, such as innovation development, internal social capital can be advantageous since it may constitute an indirect form of social control to regulate opportunistic or antisocial behaviors (Coleman, 1990b; Masciarelli, 2011). Internal social capital enhances cultural proximity and facilitates the dissemination of information and, particularly, private information that is crucial in the implementation of an innovation process.

Proposition 2a: In new technology-based ventures, the internal social capital of the founders' team increases the proximity that exists between co-founders and promotes the implementation of an innovation.

Bridging social capital refers to open networks and concerns the connecting ties formed between different groups of actors. Therefore, in our case, it refers to the links that the founders' team has with other groups outside the firm. We posit that while strong social ties with other team members (internal social capital) are advantageous for the implementation of an innovation process, the identification of the opportunity comes from a friend located outside the founders' team (external social capital). In the identification of the opportunity, a multidisciplinary effort is required. The ideas behind many innovations originate from multiple sources, and firms can benefit from access to the know-how, technology, and resources owned by external actors (Rosenberg, 1982). External social capital enables experimentation in the combination of ideas from distant sources, while internal social capital, which underpins a greater need for conformity, is more effective in supporting the implementation.

Proposition 2b: In new technology-based ventures, the external social capital of the founders' team increases the heterogeneity that exists between co-founders and promotes opportunity recognition.

The distinction between internal and external social capital is both significant and useful in the context of fostering innovation in new technology-based ventures. The presence of both internal and external social capital makes it possible to simultaneously capture the dynamics of both cultural proximity and heterogeneity within small exclusive groups (Leonard, 2004). Internal and external social capital are not mutually exclusive and the appropriate combination of the two is the optimal policy recommendation (Becker, 2004; Svendsen & Svendsen, 2004). There is an interaction effect between internal and external social capital which implies that a balance is preferred. Our discussion has an important implication for understanding the interrelations between the founders' team and the social group it belongs to. The sense of being part of a group increases the individual's propensity to share valuable knowledge and resources. Innovation processes emerge from one-to-one relationships and more specifically through continuous exchanges and cross-fertilization of ideas, notions, and technologies.

Conclusions

This chapter provides an important contribution to the existing literature. First, it contributes to the literature on the role of entrepreneurs' personality traits (Choe, Loo, & Lau, 2013; Haroon Hafeez et al., 2012; Leonelli et al., 2019) by exploring the role of personality traits considering the founders' team rather than individual entrepreneurs. Second, it contributes to the literature on social capital by highlighting the positive effects of network closure and the presence of cohesive ties – that is, internal social capital – in encouraging collaborations between actors (J. Coleman, 1988) and the benefits of intermediation opportunities created by disperse ties, that is, external social capital. The present study contributes to the debate between the two points of view on social capital, suggesting that the benefits of social capital may depend on the specific innovation stage. Internal social capital supports the implementation of innovation opportunities through shared experiences, cohesion, norms, and values that serve as substitutes for information search, control, and measurement. External social capital is relevant to identify external opportunities. In this phase of the innovation process, the benefits of social capital result from the brokerage opportunities generated by the lack of connection between separate actors (Burt, 1992). External social capital is positively associated with a firm's ability to exchange and combine different resources in ways that add value through innovative ideas.

Finally, the present chapter contributes to the literature on innovation. Social capital is confirmed to have a positive effect on the innovation process (Hauser, Tappenier, & Walde, 2007; Laursen et al., 2012; Tsai & Ghoshal, 1998), discussing how the external ties affect the innovation process. The innovation process was split into two distinct moments, and we showed how social capital differently allows for the recognition of opportunities and the implementation of innovation. This shed further light on the dynamics occurring under the influence of external forces (i.e. relationships and people) on how firms organize the innovation processes.

References

Abatecola, G. (2013). Survival or failure within the organisational life cycle. What lessons for managers? *Journal of General Management, 38*(4), 23–38.

Adler, P. S., & Kwon, S. W. (2002). Social capital: Prospects for a new concept. *The Academy of Management Review, 27*(1), 17–40.

Ahuja, G. (2000). Collaboration networks, structural holes, and innovation: A longitudinal study. *Administrative Science Quarterly, 45*(3), 355–425.

Ardichvili, A., Cardozo, R., & Ray, S. (2003). A theory of entrepreneurial opportunity identification and development. *Journal of Business Venturing, 18*(1), 105–123.

Baron, R. A., & Markman, G. D. (2003). Beyond social capital: The role of entrepreneurs' social competence in their financial success. *Journal of Business Venturing, 18*(1), 41–60.

Barringer, E., & Ireland, R. D. (2010). *Successfully launching new ventures.* London: Pearson.

Basadur, M., & Gelade, G. A. (2006). The role of knowledge management in the innovation process. *Creativity and Innovation Management, 15*(1), 45–62.

Bathelt, H., Malmberg, A., & Maskell, P. (2004). Clusters and knowledge: Local buzz, global pipelines and the process of knowledge creation. *Progress in Human Geography, 28*(1), 31–56.

Batjargal, B. (2003). Social capital and entrepreneurial performance in Russia: A longitudinal study. *Organization Studies (01708406), 24*(4), 535–556.

Batjargal, B. (2010). The effects of network's structural holes: Polycentric institutions, product portfolio, and new venture growth in China and Russia. *Strategic Entrepreneurship Journal, 4*(2), 146–163.

Baum, J. R., Frese, M., & Baron, R. A. (2014). *The psychology of entrepreneurship.* Hove, East Sussex: Psychology Press.

Baum, J. R., & Locke, E. A. (2004). The relationship of entrepreneurial traits, skill, and motivation to subsequent venture growth. *Journal of Applied Psychology, 89*(4), 587.

Becker, M. C. (2004). Organizational routines: A review of the literature. *Industrial and Corporate Change, 13*(4), 643–677.

Bollaert, H., & Petit, V. (2010). Beyond the dark side of executive psychology: Current research and new directions. *European Management Journal, 28*(5), 362–376.

Boone, C., De Brabander, B., & Van Witteloostuijn, A. (1996). CEO locus of control and small firm performance: An integrative framework and empirical test. *Journal of Management Studies, 33*(5), 667–700.

Brody, N. (2013). *Personality in search of individuality: in search of individuality.* Amsterdam: Elsevier.

Burt, R. S. (1992). *Structural holes: The social structure of competition.* Cambridge, MA: Harvard University Press.

Campbell, W. K., Goodie, A. S., & Foster, J. D. (2004). Narcissism, confidence, and risk attitude. *Journal of Behavioral Decision Making, 17*(4), 297–311.

Carpenter, M. A. (2002). The implications of strategy and social context for the relationship between top management team heterogeneity and firm performance. *Strategic Management Journal, 23*(3), 275–284.

Carpenter, M. A., Geletkanycz, M. A., & Sanders, W. G. (2004). Upper echelons research revisited: Antecedents, elements, and consequences of top management team composition. *Journal of Management, 30*(6), 749–778.

Ceci, F., Masciarelli, F., & Poledrini, S. (2019). How social capital affects innovation in a cultural network. *European Journal of Innovation Management, 15*(2), 212–231.

Chatterjee, A., & Hambrick, D. C. (2007). It's all about me: Narcissistic chief executive officers and their effects on company strategy and performance. *Administrative Science Quarterly, 52*(3), 351–386.

Child, J. (1972). Organizational structure, environment and performance: The role of strategic choice. *Sociology, 6*(1), 1–22.

Choe, K.-L., Loo, S.-C., & Lau, T.-C. (2013). Exploratory study on the relationship between entrepreneurial attitude and firm's performance. *Asian Social Science, 9*(4), 144.

Coleman, J. (1988). Social capital in the creation of human capital. *American Journal of Sociology, 94*, 95–120.

Coleman, J. S. (1990a). *Foundations of social theory.* Cambridge, MA: Harvard University Press.

Coleman, J. S. (1990b). *Social capital.* Cambridge, MA: Harvard University Press.

Colombo, M. G., Delmastro, M., & Rabbiosi, L. (2007). "High performance" work practices, decentralization, and profitability: Evidence from panel data. *Industrial and Corporate Change, 16*(6), 1037–1067.

Dakhli, M., & De Clercq, D. (2004). Human capital, social capital, and innovation: A multi-country study. *Entrepreneurship & Regional Development, 16*(2), 107–128.

Dasgupta, P., & Serageldin, I. (2000). *Social capital: A multifaceted perspective.* Washington, DC: The World Bank.

Drucker, P. F. (2002). The discipline of innovation. *Harvard Business Review, 80*(8), 95–102.

Eklinder-Frick, J., & Åge, L.-J. (2017). Perspectives on regional innovation policy–From new economic geography towards the IMP approach. *Industrial Marketing Management, 61*, 81–92.

Eklinder-Frick, J., Eriksson, L. T., & Hallén, L. (2012). Effects of social capital on processes in a regional strategic network. *Industrial Marketing Management, 41*(5), 800–806.

Eklinder-Frick, J., Eriksson, L. T., & Hallén, L. (2014). Multidimensional social capital as a boost or a bar to innovativeness. *Industrial Marketing Management, 43*(3), 460–472.

Engelen, A., Neumann, C., & Schmidt, S. (2016). Should entrepreneurially oriented firms have narcissistic CEOs? *Journal of Management, 42*(3), 698–721.

Finkelstein, S., & Hambrick, D. C. (1990). Top-management-team tenure and organizational outcomes: The moderating role of managerial discretion. *Administrative Science Quarterly, 35*, 484–503.

Florida, R. (2002). The economic geography of talent. *Annals of the Association of American Geographers, 92*(4), 743–755.

Freud, S. (2014). *On narcissism: An introduction.* Read Books Ltd.

Gabbay, S. M., & Zuckerman, E. W. (1998). Social capital and opportunity in corporate R&D: The contingent effect of contact density on mobility expectations. *Social Science Research, 27*(2), 189–217.

Gargiulo, M., & Benassi, M. (2000). Trapped in your own net? Network cohesion, structural holes, and the adaptation of social capital. *Organization Science, 11*(2), 183–196.

Gartner, W. B. (1988). "Who is an entrepreneur?" Is the wrong question. *American Journal of Small Business, 12*(4), 11–32.

Gatewood, E. J., Shaver, K. G., & Gartner, W. B. (1995). A longitudinal study of cognitive factors influencing start-up behaviors and success at venture creation. *Journal of Business Venturing, 10*(5), 371–391.

Geroski, P. A. (2000). Models of technology diffusion. *Research Policy, 29*(4), 603–625.

Gilbert, R. J. (2006). Competition and innovation. *Journal of Industrial Organization Education, 1*(1), 1–23.

Gilly, J.-P., & Torre, A. (2000). Proximity relations. Elements for an analytical framework. In M.B. Green & R.B. Mac Naughton (Eds.), *Industrial networks and proximity* (pp. 1–16). Aldershot: Ashgate.

Grabher, G. (1993). The weakness of strong ties. The lock-in of regional development in the Ruhr area. In G. Grabher (Ed.), *The embedded firm* (pp. 255–277). London and New York: Routledge.

Granovetter, M. (1973). The strength of weak ties. *American Journal of Sociology, 78*, 1360–1380.

Granovetter, M. (1983). The strength of weak ties: A network theory revisited. In P. V Marsden & N. Lin (Eds.), *Social structure and network analysis* (Vol. 1, pp. 201–233). Beverly Hills, CA: Sage.

Granovetter, M. (1985). Economic action and social structure: The problem of embeddedness. *American Journal of Sociology, 91*, 481–510.

Hambrick, D. C. (1984). Taxonomic approaches to studying strategy: Some conceptual and methodological issue. *Journal of Management, 10*(1), Spring, 27–43.

Hambrick, D. C. (2007). *Upper echelons theory: An update.* Academy of Management Briarcliff Manor, NY 10510.

Hambrick, D. C., & Mason, P. A. (1984). Upper echelon: The organization as a reflection if its top managers. *Academy of Management Review, 9*, 193–206.

Haroon Hafeez, M., Shariff, M., Noor, M., & Mad Lazim, H. (2012). Relationship between entrepreneurial orientation, firm resources, SME branding and firm's performance: Is innovation the missing link? *American Journal of Industrial and Business Management, 2*(04), 153–159.

Hauser, C., Tappenier, G., & Walde, J. (2007). The learning region: The impact of social capital and weak ties on innovation. *Regional Studies, 41*(1), 75–88.

Higgins, M. C., & Gulati, R. (2003). Getting off to a good start: The effects of upper echelon affiliations on underwriter prestige. *Organization Science, 14*(3), 244–263.

Howells, J. R. L. (2002). Tacit knowledge, innovation and economic geography. *Urban Studies, 39*(5–6), 871–884.

Hoyman, M., & Faricy, C. (2009). It takes a village: A test of the creative class, social capital, and human capital theories. *Urban Affairs Review, 44*(3), 311–333.

Inkpen, A. C., & Tsang, E. W. K. (2005). Social capital, networks, and knowledge transfer. *Academy of Management Review, 30*(1), 146–165.

Iturrioz, C., Aragón, C., & Narvaiza, L. (2015). How to foster shared innovation within SMEs' networks: Social capital and the role of intermediaries. *European Management Journal, 33*(2), 104–115.

Jacobs, J. (1961). *The death and life of great American cities.* New York: Random House.

Judge, T. A., LePine, J. A., & Rich, B. L. (2006). Loving yourself abundantly: Relationship of the narcissistic personality to self-and other perceptions of workplace deviance, leadership, and task and contextual performance. *Journal of Applied Psychology, 91*(4), 762.

Kato, M., Okamuro, H., & Honjo, Y. (2015). Does founders' human capital matter for innovation? Evidence from Japanese start-ups. *Journal of Small Business Management, 53*(1), 114–128.

Keck, S. L. (1997). Top management team structure: Differential effects by environmental context. *Organization Science, 8*(2), 143–156.

Kickul, J., & Gundry, L. (2002). Prospecting for strategic advantage: The proactive entrepreneurial personality and small firm innovation. *Journal of Small Business Management, 40*(2), 85–97.

Kickul, J., & Walters, J. (2002). Recognizing new opportunities and innovations. *International Journal of Entrepreneurial Behavior & Research, 8*(6), 292–308.

King, L. A., Walker, L. M., & Broyles, S. J. (1996). Creativity and the five-factor model. *Journal of Research in Personality, 30*(2), 189–203.

Knack, S., & Keefer, P. (1997). Does social capital have an economic payoff? A cross-country investigation. *Quarterly Journal of Economics, 112*(4), 1251–1288.

Knight, D., Pearce, C. L., Smith, K. G., Olian, J. D., Sims, H. P., Smith, K. A., & Flood, P. (1999). Top management team diversity, group process, and strategic consensus. *Strategic Management Journal, 20*(5), 445–465.

Knoben, J., & Oerlemans, L. A. G. (2006). Proximity and inter-organizational collaboration: A literature review. *International Journal of Management Reviews, 8*(2), 71–89.

Krause, D. R., Handfield, R. B., & Tyler, B. B. (2007). The relationships between supplier development, commitment, social capital accumulation and performance improvement. *Journal of Operations Management, 25*(2), 528–545.

Laursen, K., Masciarelli, F., & Prencipe, A. (2012). Trapped or spurred by the home region? The effects of potential social capital on involvement in foreign markets for goods and technology. *Journal of International Business Studies, 43*, 783–807.

Lazega, E. (2009). Cooperation among competitors. Its social mechanisms through network analyses. *Sociologica, 3*(1), 0.

Lee, D. Y., Tsang, E. W. K., & Littunen, H. (2001). Entrepreneurship and the characteristics of the entrepreneurial personality. *International Journal of Entrepreneurial Behavior & Research, 38*(4), 583–602.

Leonard, M. (2004). Bonding and bridging social capital: Reflections from Belfast. *Sociology, 38*(5), 927–944.

Leonelli, S., Ceci, F., & Masciarelli, F. (2016). The importance of entrepreneurs' traits in explaining start-ups' innovativeness. *Sinergie Italian Journal of Management, 34*(Sep-Dec), 71–85.

Leonelli, S., Ceci, F., & Masciarelli, F. (2019). "I am apt to show off": Exploring the relationship between entrepreneurs' narcissism and start-up innovation. *Sinergie Italian Journal of Management, 37*(3), 39–61.

Leonelli, S., & Masciarelli, F. (2019). Market scenarios and start-up's patenting: The moderator role of entrepreneurs'narcissism. Thessaloniki, Greece: *12th Annual Conference of the EuroMed Academy of Business.*

Leonelli, S., Masciarelli, F., & Fontana, F. (2019). The impact of personality traits and abilities on entrepreneurial orientation in SMEs. *Journal of Small Business & Entrepreneurship*, 1–26. doi:10.1080/08276331.2019.1666339.

Littunen, H. (2000). Entrepreneurship and the characteristics of the entre-preneurial personality. *International Journal of Entrepreneurial Behavior & Research, 6*(6), 295–310.

Maccoby, M. (2003). *The productive narcissist: The promise and peril of visionary leadership.* New York: Broadway Books.

Maine, E., Soh, P.-H., & Dos Santos, N. (2015). The role of entrepreneurial decision-making in opportunity creation and recognition. *Technovation, 39*, 53–72.

Masciarelli, F. (2011). *The strategic value of social capital: How firms capitalise on social assets.* Cheltenham: Edward Elgar Publishing.

McPherson, M., Smith-Lovin, L., & Cook, J. M. (2001). Birds of a feather: Homophily in social networks. *Annual Review of Sociology, 27*(1), 415–444.

Milliken, F. J., & Martins, L. L. (1996). Searching for common threads: Understanding the multiple effects of diversity in organizational groups. *Academy of Management Review, 21*(2), 402–433.

Molina-Morales, F. X., García-Villaverde, P. M., & Parra-Requena, G. (2014). Geographical and cognitive proximity effects on innovation performance in SMEs: A way through knowledge acquisition. *International Entrepreneurship and Management Journal, 10*(2), 231–251.

Morgan, K. (2004). The exaggerated death of geography: Learning, proximity and territorial innovation systems. *Journal of Economic Geography, 4*, 3–21.

Mu, J., Peng, G., & Love, E. (2008). Interfirm networks, social capital, and knowledge flow. *Journal of Knowledge Management, 12*(4), 86–100.

Nga, J. K. H., & Shamuganathan, G. (2010). The influence of personality traits and demographic factors on social entrepreneurship start up intentions. *Journal of Business Ethics, 95*(2), 259–282.

Nooteboom, B. (1994). Innovation and diffusion in small firms: Theory and evidence. *Small Business Economics, 6*(5), 327–347.

O'Reilly, C. A., Caldwell, D. F., Chatman, J. A., & Doerr, B. (2014). The promise and problems of organizational culture: CEO personality, culture, and firm performance. *Group & Organization Management, 39*(6), 595–625.

Padgett, J., & Powell, W. (2011). *The emergence of organizations and markets.* Princeton, New Jersey: Princeton University Press.

Parmigiani, A., & Rivera-Santos, M. (2011). Clearing a path through the forest: A meta-review of interorganizational relationships. *Journal of Management, 37*(4), 1108–1136.

Patterson, F. (1999). *Innovation potential predictor.* Oxford: Oxford Psychologists Press.

Patterson, F. (2002). Great minds don't think alike? Person-level predictors of innovation at work. *International Review of Industrial and Organizational Psychology, 17*, 115–144.

Patulny, R. V, & Svendsen, G. L. H. (2007). Exploring the social capital grid: Bonding, bridging, qualitative, quantitative. *International Journal of Sociology and Social Policy, 27*(1/2), 32–51.

Pelled, L. H. (1996). Demographic diversity, conflict, and work group outcomes: An intervening process theory. *Organization Science, 7*(6), 615–631.

Pérez-Luño, A., Medina, C. C., Lavado, A. C., & Rodríguez, G. C. (2011). How social capital and knowledge affect innovation. *Journal of Business Research, 64*(12), 1369–1376.

Perry-Smith, J. E., & Mannucci, P. V. (2017). From creativity to innovation: The social network drivers of the four phases of the idea journey. *Academy of Management Review, 42*(1), 53–79.

Petit, V., & Bollaert, H. (2012). Flying too close to the sun? Hubris among CEOs and how to prevent it. *Journal of Business Ethics, 108*(3), 265–283.

Pitcher, P., & Smith, A. D. (2001). Top management team heterogeneity: Personality, power, and proxies. *Organization Science, 12*(1), 1–18.

Plummer, J. T. (2000). How personality makes a difference. *Journal of Advertising Research, 40*(6), 79–83.

Portes, A. (1998). Social capital: Its origins and applications in modern sociology. *Annual Review of Sociology, 24*, 1–24.

Powell, W. W., Koput, K. W., & Smith-Doerr, L. (1996). Interorganizational collaboration and the locus of innovation: Networks of learning in biotechnology. *Administrative Science Quarterly, 41*, 116–145.

Putnam, R. D. (1993). The prosperous community: Social capital and public life. *The American Prospect, 13*(4), 35–42.

Putnam, R. D. (2000). *Bowling alone* (S. & Schuste, Ed.). New York: Palgrave Macmillan.

Rauch, A., & Frese, M. (2007). Born to be an entrepreneur? Revisiting the personality approach to entrepreneurship. In J. R. Baum, M. Frese, & R. A. Baron (Eds.), *The Psychology of Entrepreneurship* (pp. 41–65). Mahwah: Lawrence Erlbaum Associates.

Rogers, E. M. (2010). *Diffusion of innovations.* New York: Simon and Schuster.

Rosenberg, N. (1982). Inside the black box. In *Technology and economics.* (pp. 156–157). New York: Cambridge University Press.

Rosenthal, S. A., & Pittinsky, T. L. (2006). Narcissistic leadership. *The Leadership Quarterly, 17*(6), 617–633.

Rosenthal, S., & Strange, C. (2003). Geography, industrial organization, and agglomeration. *Review of Economics and Statistics, 85*(2), 377–393.

Sajuria, J., vanHeerde-Hudson, J., Hudson, D., Dasandi, N., & Theocharis, Y. (2015). Tweeting alone? An analysis of bridging and bonding social capital in online networks. *American Politics Research, 43*(4), 708–738.

Sarasvathy, S. D., Dew, N., Velamuri, S. R., & Venkataraman, S. (2003). Three views of entrepreneurial opportunity. In *Handbook of entrepreneurship research.* In Z.J Acs & D. B. Audretsch (Eds.) (pp. 141–160). Switzerland: Springer.

Shane, S., & Venkataraman, S. (2000). The promise of entrepreneurship as a field of research. *Academy of Management Review, 25*(1), 217–226.

Shane, S., Venkataraman, S., & MacMillan, I. (1995). Cultural differences in innovation championing strategies. *Journal of Management, 21*(5), 931–952.

Simons, T., Pelled, L. H., & Smith, K. A. (1999). Making use of difference: Diversity, debate, and decision comprehensiveness in top management teams. *Academy of Management Journal, 42*(6), 662–673.

Simsek, Z., Heavey, C., & Veiga, J. (Jack) F. (2010). The impact of CEO core self-evaluation on the firm's entrepreneurial orientation. *Strategic Management Journal, 31*(1), 110–119.

Soetanto, D., Huang, Q., & Jack, S. (2018). Obstacles, networking approaches and entrepreneurial network changes. *European Management Review, 15*(2), 171–189.

Svendsen, G. L. H., & Svendsen, G. T. (2004). *The creation and destruction of social capital: Entrepreneurship, co-operative movements, and institutions.* Cheltenham:Edward Elgar Publishing.

Tidd, J. (1995). Development of novel products through intraorganizational and interorganizational networks. *Journal of Product Innovation Management, 12*(4), 307–322.

Tsai, W., & Ghoshal, S. (1998). Social capital and value creation: The role of intrafirm networks. *Academy of Management Journal, 41*(4), 464–476.

Uzzi, B. (1997). Social structure and competition in interfirm networks: The paradox of embeddedness. *Administrative Science Quarterly, 42*, 35–67.

Venkataraman, S. (1997). *The distinctive domain of entrepreneurship research.* Seminal ideas for the next twenty-five years of advances, *3* 5–20.

Wales, W. J., Patel, P. C., & Lumpkin, G. T. (2013). In pursuit of greatness: CEO narcissism, entrepreneurial orientation, and firm performance variance. *Journal of Management Studies, 50*(6), 1041–1069.

Webber, S. S., & Donahue, L. M. (2001). Impact of highly and less job-related diversity on work group cohesion and performance: A meta-analysis. *Journal of Management, 27*(2), 141–162.

West, J., & Bogers, M. (2014). Leveraging external sources of innovation: A review of research on open innovation. *Journal of Product Innovation Management, 31*(4), 814–831.

Wiersema, M. F., & Bantel, K. A. (1992). Top management team demography and corporate strategic change. *Academy of Management Journal, 35*(1), 91–121.

Wuyts, S., Colombo, M. G., Dutta, S., & Nooteboom, B. (2005). Empirical tests of optimal cognitive distance. *Journal of Economic Behavior & Organization, 58*(2), 277–302.

Zhao, H., Seibert, S. E., & Lumpkin, G. T. (2010). The relationship of personality to entrepreneurial intentions and performance: A meta-analytic review. *Journal of Management, 36*(2), 381–404.

Part Two
Applications

4 Proximity Outside Organizations

A Study on Inter-organization Networks

Introduction

In this chapter, we examine the impact of cultural diversity and proximity in an interorganizational network, with a particular focus on the following elements: innovation process and entrepreneurial learning. The investigation is based on the study of a unique case; however, two analyses have been carried out, using different methods and perspectives.

In order to understand how firms exploit their cultural network to manage their innovation processes and how being part of a cultural network affects entrepreneurial learning, we will focus on a unique empirical setting: the local branch of an international entrepreneurial association, which is referred to as the "Association" to preserve its anonymity. The Association started its activity in 1986 as a network of entrepreneurs who intended to share their human and economic resources for their mutual benefit. The entrepreneurs joining the Association share the norms, principles, and values of the Roman Catholic Church. Currently, the Association has 38 branches in Italy and 17 abroad, it counts over 36,000 members - mainly profit-making firms. The Association is configured as a cohesive network of firms and, by means of various socialization mechanisms such as social gatherings and meetings, it encourages members' identification with the network and their adherence to a set of common norms, principles, and values. Its members constitute "a community with shared interests, a common identity, and a commitment to the common good" (Adler & Kwon, 2002, p. 25). Previous studies carried out on the same network confirm the suitability of this network as an ideal context for the study of a cultural network (Ceci, Masciarelli, & Poledrini, 2019; Ceci, Masciarelli, & Prencipe, 2016; Ceci & Prencipe, 2019). These studies highlighted how cultural values influence knowledge sharing in a network of firms, as well as the effect of the entrepreneur's personal beliefs on the possibility to learn from such a network and, therefore, improve his or her firm's performance. The cohesion defining the network is particularly evident among the members of the Association's local branches. The Association, therefore, represents an example of a cultural network, that is, a network characterized by actors connecting and sharing the same norms, principles, and values and by their trust in the collective authority, which is the repository of common values (Eklinder-Frick et al., 2014).

Innovation Process and Cultural Proximity

The first aspect that we intend to examine while looking at the effect of cultural proximity is its impact on the innovation process. As widely theorized, the innovation process can be structured in two phases and it involves (i) the recognition of new opportunities and (ii) the implementation of new ideas into actions (Maine, Soh, & Dos Santos, 2015; Perry-Smith & Mannucci, 2017; Rogers, 2010). The recognition of opportunities is the first step in the innovation process and it consists in the ability to find a new and profitable business (Barringer & Ireland, 2010), to identify a new market need or to creatively combine resources to provide a higher added value (Ardichvili, Cardozo, & Ray, 2003). Furthermore, opportunities may arise as a result of industrial or technological changes or unforeseen events in a particular market (Drucker, 2002). The second phase is the implementation and it refers to the application of ideas that have already been generated. It involves the transformation of the new idea into a product or process innovation. Therefore, the implementation of an innovation involves development (adaptation of scientific knowledge aimed at meeting a potential customer or user demand), commercialization (production stage leading to the distribution of the new product or service), and diffusion/adoption (the innovation circulates and reaches potential adopters) (Rogers, 2010).

To explore the innovation process, we have drawn on the empirical context described above. The primary source of data is represented by the open-ended interviews, where the researchers ask for the interviewee's views on specific topics (Oppenheim, 2000). These interviews were based on a semi-structured questionnaire. To explore the benefits of cultural proximity at different stages of the innovation process, the concept of social capital will be taken as a basis. More specifically, we will look into its two different dimensions: bonding and bridging social capital (Putnam, 2000): bonding social capital refers to internal connections within the group; bridging social capital refers to connections with actors outside the group (Adler & Kwon, 2002). Bonding is built upon internal relationships, which foster trust, cohesion, and common understanding among group members (Adler & Kwon, 2002; Nahapiet & Ghoshal, 1998; Woolcock & Narayan, 2000). Bridging social capital refers to open networks that are "outward looking and encompass people across diverse social cleavages" (Putnam, 2000, p. 22). Vissa (2012) claims that entrepreneurs increase their bridging social capital by expanding the network, which includes reaching out to new contacts and being outward-looking, connecting to a number of individuals and building reciprocity with various groups of individuals (Smith, Smith, & Shaw, 2017; Williams, 2006).

Opportunity Recognition and Bridging Social Capital

To explore how cultural proximity is linked to the recognition of opportunities and the implementation of innovations, we will discuss how firms can take advantage of their cultural network to recognize new opportunities. Our findings show that bridging social capital enhances firm's ability to recognize new opportunities. Bridging social capital builds on the notion of what network scholars refer to as weak ties, which are loose connections between actors that may provide mutual formal support but, typically, do not provide emotional support, as the following extract shows: "We are here at the fair to meet, so we try to make the most of this opportunity to communicate, then to inquire and look for new relationships." Here, the interviewee emphasizes that the search for new opportunities takes place outside the inner circle, strategically relying on the bridging social capital.

Although the majority of the interviewees recognized the importance of bridging social capital in the identification of new ideas, some of them also pointed to limitations and drawbacks arising from the reliance on bridging relations. In fact, one interviewee said: "But I think this is the only occasion when we tried to implement an idea, since we did not have all the success that we were expecting. We collected many ideas, but we got zero results." This finding suggests that bridging alone is not sufficient for a successful innovation process. In addition, another interviewee stressed the lack of appropriate incentives in a bridging context: "However, in my opinion, it is sometimes necessary to have stronger stimuli to be able to catalyze in the research and development something coming from the network." Note that bridging social capital, although effective for promoting the identification of ideas and the recognition of opportunities, does not, without the appropriate incentives, ensure a successful innovation process since the risk of failure remains very high.

According to our findings, in the case of opportunity recognition, when firms are able to build new scientific and technological knowledge or propose new business ideas, the involvement of partners from different backgrounds outside the cultural networks is advantageous in the early stages of the innovation process. Many innovations arise from firms being able to gain access to different know-how, technologies, and resources from multiple sources. Bridging social capital helps firms to acquire knowledge that is not available within the network, while bonding social capital, by imposing a greater need for conformity and granting access to more redundant information, is not beneficial for identifying new opportunities.

Innovation Implementation and Bonding Social Capital

After the identification of new opportunities, the next step in the innovation process requires decisions regarding the most appropriate production processes, technologies, and suppliers to involve. Our data suggest that entrepreneurs rely on the people they know best and can be trusted. In fact, bonding social capital refers to the connections and activities taking place within a network, and it is based on trust, cohesion, and a common understanding among members. The following interview extract clarifies the circumstances where bonding social capital can be exploited: "He (i.e. a partner in an innovative project) saw our reality, he saw the people surrounding us as a firm; we (i.e. local branch members) are a small group that can perform nicely. (...) We then presented a spin-off." The same interviewee added: "Here (i.e. within the local branch) everything is easier since there is a relationship among people. We trust each other, there is nothing hidden here, we can count on maximum transparency. Everything is decided together." However, when it comes to developing new ideas, bonding social capital does not seem to be effective, as one of the interviewees pointed put: "We have created a group of people operating in completely different areas, but we are trying to put ideas together and then see how we can put them into practice." This extract proves the need for multidisciplinary information to facilitate technology brokerage that bonding social capital does not guarantee.

Our results show that, in the case of implementing an innovation, the involvement of partners belonging to the same cultural network is advantageous. Therefore, bonding social capital, by enabling firms to engage in mutual knowledge exchange, lowers the scarcity of resources, facilitates technological specialization, and reduces the risks associated with the implementation of a research project.

The bridging/bonding distinction is not mutually exclusive. Both types of social capital, in fact, interact in a continuum of activities resulting in an organic and coherent innovation process. These two dimensions capture both openness and closedness dynamics, as shown in the following extract:

> Now we are collaborating (i.e. with another local member) and we have requested some information from another firm linked to our Association network (i.e. a member not belonging to the local branch). We asked his opinion, his thoughts concerning the suppliers' market: they know the global market for kiwi (i.e. one of the main raw materials needed for the business), so we asked for some information about the pomegranate market (i.e. another raw material needed for the business). (...) During the second exploratory meeting, they (i.e. the local branch members) showed interest in being part of the project. This supported and encouraged me, since this could clearly represent a good idea and an opportunity.

The above extract shows that collaboration is crucial at every stage of the innovation process - from the identification of an opportunity to the implementation of an innovation. The two components of social capital are both present: successful innovation is the result of the interplay between bonding and bridging social capital, exploited at the appropriate stage.

Our study confirms that sharing culture and values has a positive effect on the innovation process (Hauser, Tappenier, & Walde, 2007; Laursen, Masciarelli, & Prencipe, 2012a; Tsai & Ghoshal, 1998), and provides an important contribution to the existing work in this field. Bonding social capital is shown to foster the implementation of innovation while bridging social capital proves to be more effective in the generation phase. We add to the literature on social capital by showing that bonding social capital through group cohesion, common scope, and vision; shared norms and values; collective actions; and trust has a strong impact on the implementation of innovation. This finding contributes to the research that underlines the importance of community-level social capital (Coleman, 1990; Laursen, Masciarelli, & Prencipe, 2012b; Putnam, 1993). A deep sense of community, shared values, and norms are transferred from the individual sphere to the work context and support risky decisions such as those related to the innovation process. Shared experiences, cohesion, norms, and values act as substitutes for the research, control, and measurement of information, and promote the innovation process.

Entrepreneurial Learning, Cultural Compatibility, Identity, Shared Creativity: An Exploration of How Spirituality Affects Cultural Proximity

The second aspect worth considering when looking at the effect of cultural proximity is its impact on entrepreneurial learning. The focus here is on the micro-foundations of cultural proximity facilitators and the role played by shared beliefs. More specifically, the role played by spirituality is explored. Spirituality is increasingly used to define the personal and subjective aspects of religious experience (Hill & Pargament, 2008), and it is an object of academic debate (Neubert, Bradley, Ardianti, & Simiyu, 2017; Putnam, Campbell, & Garrett, 2012). A number of studies focus on the impact that spirituality has on different fields of human endeavor, ranging from individual well-being and behavior (Lim & Putnam, 2010), entrepreneurial attitude (Carswell & Rolland, 2004; Christopher, 2011; Davis, 2013; Dragunova, 2006; Roessingh & Boersma, 2011) to broader aspects such as economic growth (Barro & McCleary, 2003; Neubert et al., 2017). Spirituality is claimed to affect the cultural proximity of entrepreneurs operating within a firm network and, accordingly, it can affect network-based learning.

Spirituality and religious beliefs play a role in determining economic outcomes (Carswell & Rolland, 2004; Guiso, Sapienza, & Zingales, 2003; Lim & Putnam, 2010): the Protestant Reformation is a clear example. It changed the way people thought about the pursuit of wealth, which was not just about personal gain, but was also a duty of the individual (Rietveld & Van Burg, 2014; Swedberg, 2000; Weber, 1904). This change had a profound impact on individual behaviors, making it legitimate for the bourgeoisie to disrupt the existing order and introduce a new one based on individual opportunities to achieve prosperity. Guiso, Sapienza, and Zingales

(2003) consider the effect of religion on trust and find that individuals who regularly attend religious services show much higher levels of trust towards other individuals. Spear (2010) reports several cases (e.g. Quakers in nineteenth-century England or the Protestant network in Latin America) where belonging to a cohesive group having strong religious connotations facilitated the development of new business ideas, suggesting the existence of a connection between religious values, culture, and economic practices. Roessingh and Boersma (2011) described how the specific religious background of social groups influence and drive a process of organizational change, thus shaping the development path followed by a community (Christopher, 2011; Roessingh & Boersma, 2011; Roessingh & Nuijten, 2012). Saxenian (1994) showed that entrepreneurs working in Silicon Valley tend to use their social networks to connect with investors, and religious individuals consider their religious group as the most important cultural network (English-Lueck & Saveri, 2001). Literature also examined the benefits in terms of belonging to an information network. In this situation, information networks mainly consist of informal sources such as colloquies, friends, peers, and co-religionists. More specifically, being part of a religious group affects the amount of information and support that can also be obtained from a business point of view (Altinay, 2008; Boissevain, Grotenbreg, Goffee, & Scale, 1987; Dana, 2006).

Networking enables firms to build high-quality connections, thus allowing a more effective knowledge exchange and faster learning (Andersson, Forsgren, & Holm, 2002; Carmeli & Azeroual, 2009; Schulz, 2001; Sorenson, Rivkin, & Fleming, 2006; Yli-Renko, Autio, & Sapienza, 2001). Network-based learning is defined as the rate at which a firm learns through the acquisition of knowledge facilitated by being a member of a network (Lane & Lubatkin, 1998; Lavie, 2006). Network-based learning arises from a high level of interconnection and interaction among the firms in a network (Lavie, 2006; Nahapiet & Ghoshal, 1998). High levels of interconnection and interaction are observed in those networks where firms have similar organizational norms, values, expectations, and systems of meaning and consider themselves as being part of a social group (Adler & Kwon, 2002; Kambil, Eselius, & Monteiro, 2000; Lazoi, Ceci, Corallo, & Secundo, 2011; Madhok & Tallman, 1998; Nahapiet & Ghoshal, 1998; Tajfel & Turner, 2004). In order to investigate the role of the antecedents to network-based learning, we developed a model comprising three mediators, namely cultural compatibility, identity, and shared creativity, which we will discuss in turn below. Figure 4.1 is a graphical representation that highlights the mediating roles of cultural compatibility, identity, and shared creativity norms as three elements that can define cultural proximity.

Cultural compatibility or congruence of organizational philosophies, objectives, and values among network members influences the extent to which members are able to achieve their synergistic potential (Madhok & Tallman, 1998). This dimension addresses broad issues related to organizational norms and value systems. Cultural incompatibility can result in an inability to develop a harmonious relationship, thus having a negative impact on collaborative effectiveness (Sarkar, Cavusgil, & Evirgen, 1997). It is expected that, in networks having high cultural proximity, entrepreneurs will be more likely to share organizational philosophies with other network members. Cultural compatibility fosters knowledge sharing and the development of a common language among network members and promotes network-based learning (Sarkar et al., 1997).

When discussing the "identity" of the mediator, reference should be made to the Social Identity Theory which argues that individuals can define themselves as being part of more than one social group (e.g. profession, family, company) (Ashforth, Johnson, Hogg, & Terry, 2001; Meyer, Becker, & Van Dick, 2007; Tajfel & Turner,

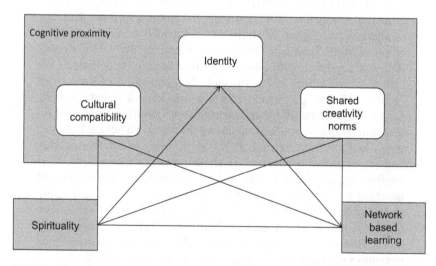

Figure 4.1 Analytical model.

2004). A central aspect of this theory lies in the relationship and potential conflict among multiple work-related identities – for example, on a professional, organizational, networking level. In large firm networks, some members may be far from their headquarters, thus perceiving themselves as being "out of sight, out of mind" (Wiesenfeld, Raghuram, & Garud, 2001, p. 214). In such networks, dual affiliation (to both the firm and the network) may increase the ambiguity of network identity. Network members from different firms will be more likely to have different professional experience and different backgrounds (e.g. Gurung & Prater, 2006). High levels of cultural compatibility have a positive effect on identity by reducing the role played by work experience and background (see e.g. Roessingh & Boersma, 2011). A strong identity has also a positive effect on network-based learning by increasing trust among members and the willingness to share knowledge and information.

The last mediator is represented by 'shared creativity'. Shared creativity norms refer to expectations, interpretations, and systems of meaning that capture firms' shared language and codes (Nahapiet & Ghoshal, 1998). These norms result from firm behavior (individual and collective), which creates cultural compatibility between partnering firms and informs and governs knowledge sharing (Adler and Kwon, 2002). Shared creativity norms reflect shared beliefs, practices, and the common ground characterizing the nature of cooperation among firms within a network (Nahapiet & Ghoshal, 1998). Shared creativity norms help promote cultural compatibility among firms, inform and shape their cooperation, and provide a basis for continuous interactions (Ceci & D'Andrea, 2014; Hughes, Morgan, Ireland, & Hughes, 2011; Hughes, Morgan, Ireland, & Hughes, 2014). Over time, these norms increasingly operate at the network level, thus representing an institutionalized set of rules that govern behavior and eliminating the need for formal contracts (Gulati, Nohria, & Zaheer, 2000). These rules act as a governance mechanism which facilitates knowledge transfer.

The development of common creativity norms within network members has been suggested by Kambil, Eselius, and Monteiro (2000) as a catalyst for firm's entrepreneurial abilities to generate more learning. Reduced search times tend to increase this effect. In a network based on religious values, entrepreneurs having high levels of spirituality are likely to have similar standards as other network members. Furthermore, the existence of implicit norms and rules operating at the network level, established and guided by the network itself, also facilitates knowledge exchange since opportunism would be severely sanctioned (Inkpen & Tsang, 2005).

Based on quantitative data collected through a survey, Partial Least Squares (SmartPLS v.3.2.1) (Ringle, Wende, & Becker, 2015) were used to estimate our model. First, individual item reliability was assessed by examining the loadings of measures on their respective constructs. Table 4.1 provides the final list of the individual items used in the analysis, as well as their loadings. Overall, these statistics are above the cut-off value suggested, thus indicating that all of our items exhibit good individual item reliability. Then, the adequacy of the measurement model was assessed by examining individual item reliabilities, along with convergent and discriminant validity. Table 4.2 presents the internal consistency values for the constructs, and the correlation matrix between these constructs, with the diagonal indicating the square root of the average variance extracted. Table 4.3 reports the results of the structural model.

Table 4.1 Measurement model

Construct	Item[a]	Loading
Spirituality	Religious people are more likely to maintain moral standards	0.670
	Belief in a religion helps one understand the meaning of life	0.774
	Belief in religion makes people good citizens	0.685
	Religious faith contributes to good mental health	0.809
	There is a supreme being controlling the universe	0.747
Cultural compatibility	The organizational values and social norms prevalent in the associated firms were congruent	0.753
	Executives from associated firms involved in this project have compatible philosophies / approaches to business dealings	0.678
	The goals and objectives of associated firms were compatible with each other	0.789
	The chemistry was right between the associated firms	0.797
	Both my firm and the other firms associated with the association have a similar philosophy and approach to business	0.815
	There is a lot in common in the way we do business	0.559

Construct	Item[a]	Loading
Identity	When someone criticizes the association, I take it personally	0.819
	I care much what others think of association	0.736
	When I speak of the association, usually I use 'we' instead of 'their'	0.730
	When someone praises the association, I feel it like a personal compliment	0.899
	The successes of the association are my successes	0.830
Shared creativity norms	Businesses in the association share a common feeling of creativity	0.712
	A creative and vibrant atmosphere exists within the association	0.922
	There is an innovative 'feel' throughout the association	0.894
	The association generates a creative environment to explore and experiment	0.776
Network-based learning	Operating in this association has provided a fast way of learning	0.783
	Our rate of learning is far ahead of where we would be had we 'gone it alone'	0.761
	The quality of knowledge and experiences gained is superior to what we would have achieved had we 'gone it alone'	0.754
	Exchange of information and experiences takes place frequently and informally among the members of the association	0.752
	We have learned a great deal from the members of the association	0.835

a   Scale ranging from 1 (strongly disagree) to 5 (strongly agree).

Table 4.2 Construct-level measurement statistics and correlation of constructs

Construct	Internal consistency	Spirituality	Cultural compatibility	Identity	Shared creativity norms	Network-based learning
Spirituality	0.857	**0.546**[a]				
Cultural compatibility	0.876	0.253	**0.544**			
Identity	0.902	0.390	0.501	**0.648**		
Shared creativity norms	0.898	0.323	0.727	0.618	**0.689**	
Network-based learning	0.857	0.245	0.721	0.617	0.709	**0.605**

a   Diagonal elements in bold are square roots of average variance extracted.

Table 4.3 Effect of spirituality on network-based learning: standardized PLS coefficients

Dependent variable	Independent variable	H	Hypothesized sign	Standardized coefficient[a]	
Network-based learning	Spirituality	Hp1	+	−0.048	
	Cultural Compatibility	Hp 2b	+	0.407	***
	Identity	Hp 3b	+	0.270	**
	Shared Creativity Norms	Hp 4b	+	0.262	*
Cultural compatibility	Spirituality	Hp 2a	+	0.253	**
Identity	Spirituality	Hp 3a	+	0.390	***
Shared creativity norms	Spirituality	Hp 4a	+	0.323	***

a *Significant at the 0.10 level. **Significant at the 0.05 level. ***Significant at the 0.01 level.

The results indicate that spirituality is positively related to cultural compatibility (β = .253, p < .05), identity (β = .390, p < .01), and shared creativity norms (β = .323, p < .01). The results also show positive relationships between cultural compatibility and network-based learning (β = .407, p < .01), identity and network-based learning (β = .270, p < .01), and shared creativity norms and network-based learning (β = .262, p < .10). Finally, the effect of spirituality on network-based learning is not statistically significant (β = −0.048, p > 0.1). However, the relationship between spirituality (the independent variable) and cultural compatibility, identity and shared creativity norms (the mediators) is both positive and significant (β = .253 p <. 05; Hp 3a: β =.390, p < .01; Hp4a: β = .323, p < .01). Also, the mediating effect of cultural compatibility, identity, and shared creativity norms on network-based learning (the dependent variable) is significant (β = .407, p < .01; Hp 3b: β = .270, p < .01; Hp 4b: β = .262, p < .10). Therefore, spirituality is shown to indirectly affect network-based learning through cultural compatibility, identity, and shared creativity norms.

By means of this empirical investigation, we explored how cultural proximity can facilitate firms' learning ability. The results of our mediated model confirm that spirituality (in a network characterized by shared religious norms) is positively related to cultural compatibility, identity, and shared creativity norms. The effect of spirituality on network-based learning is not statistically significant, while the mediating effect of cultural compatibility, identity, and shared creativity norms on network-based learning is significant. Therefore, spirituality indirectly influences network-based learning through cultural compatibility, identity, and shared creativity norms. In this chapter, the role of cultural proximity in enabling learning is highlighted. More specifically, a common spiritual view is shown to have a positive effect on the possibility to improve learning experiences within a network. The cultural proximity of entrepreneurs is a factor that promotes the development of cultural compatibility and identity within the group, and shared creativity norms affect important managerial processes such as the learning ability of the firm.

References

Adler, P. S., & Kwon, S. W. (2002). Social capital: Prospects for a new concept. *The Academy of Management Review, 27*(1), 17–40.

Altinay, L. (2008). The relationship between an entrepreneur's culture and the entrepreneurial behaviour of the firm. *Journal of Small Business and Enterprise Development, 15*(1), 111–129.

Andersson, U., Forsgren, M., & Holm, U. (2002). The strategic impact of external networks: Subsidiary performance and competence development in the multinational corporation. *Strategic Management Journal, 23*(11), 979–996.

Ardichvili, A., Cardozo, R., & Ray, S. (2003). A theory of entrepreneurial opportunity identification and development. *Journal of Business Venturing, 18*(1), 105–123.

Ashforth, B. E., Johnson, S. A., Hogg, M. A., & Terry, D. J. (2001). Which hat to wear. In Hogg, M. A.,& Terry D.J. *Social Identity processes in organizational contexts*, Philadelphia, PA: Psychology Press, 32–48.

Barringer, E., & Ireland, R. D. (2010). *Successfully launching new ventures.* New Jersey, US, Pearson.

Barro, R. J., & McCleary, R. (2003). *Religion and economic growth.* No. w10147 National Bureau of Economic Research.

Basadur, M., & Gelade, G. A. (2006). The role of knowledge management in the innovation process. *Creativity and Innovation Management, 15*(1), 45–62.

Boissevain, J., Grotenbreg, H., Goffee, R., & Scale, R. (1987). Ethnic enterprise in the Netherlands. The surinamese of Amsterdam, London, UK, Routledge

Carmeli, A., & Azeroual, B. (2009). How relational capital and knowledge combination capability enhance the performance of work units in a high technology industry. *Strategic Entrepreneurship Journal, 3*(1), 85–103.

Carswell, P., & Rolland, D. (2004). The role of religion in entrepreneurship participation and perception. *International Journal of Entrepreneurship and Small Business, 1*(3–4), 280–286.

Ceci, F., & D'Andrea, D. (2014). Knowledge dynamics in fragmented industries. *International Journal of Innovation and Technology Management, 11*(2), 145004–145032.

Ceci, F., Masciarelli, F., & Poledrini, S. (2019). How social capital affects innovation in a cultural network: Exploring the role of bonding and bridging social capital. *European Journal of Innovation Management.* ahead-of-print.

Ceci, F., Masciarelli, F., & Prencipe, A. (2016). Entrepreneurial learning in a network: The role of cultural values. In Passiante G. & Romano A. *Creating Technology-Driven Entrepreneurship* (pp. 221–240). Palgrave Macmillan, London Springer.

Ceci, F., & Prencipe, A. (2019). Is there a supreme being controlling the universe? Entrepreneurs' personal beliefs and their impact on network learning. *International Journal of Entrepreneurship and Small Business, 38*(3), 359–378.

Christopher, C. A. (2011). Religion in entrepreneurship: How international and indigenous Indian entrepreneurs differ. *International Journal of Entrepreneurship and Small Business, 13*(4), 411–428.

Coleman, J. S. (1990). *Social capital.* Cambridge, MA: Harvard University Press.

Dana, L. P. (2006). A historical study of the traditional livestock merchants of Alsace. *British Food Journal, 108*(7), 586–598.

Davis, M. K. (2013). Entrepreneurship: An Islamic perspective. *International Journal of Entrepreneurship and Small Business, 20*(1), 63–69.

Dragunova, E. (2006). National features of Russian entrepreneurs. *International Journal of Entrepreneurship and Small Business, 3*(5), 607–620.

Drucker, P. F. (2002). The discipline of innovation. *Harvard Business Review, 80*(8), 95–102.

English-Lueck, J. A., & Saveri, A. (2001). Silicon missionaries and identity evangelists. *Anthropology of Work Review, 22*(1), 7–12.

Eklinder-Frick, J., Eriksson L. T., & Hallén L. (2014)Multidimensional social capital as a boost or a bar to innovativeness. *Industrial Marketing Management* 43.3: 460–472.

Guiso, L., Sapienza, P., & Zingales, L. (2003). People's opium? Religion and economic attitudes. *Journal of Monetary Economics, 50*(1), 225–282.

Gulati, R., Nohria, N., & Zaheer, A. (2000). Guest editors' introduction to the special issue: Strategic networks. *Strategic Management Journal, 21*(3), 199–201.

Gurung, A., & Prater, E. (2006). A research framework for the impact of cultural differences on IT outsourcing. *Journal of Global Information Technology Management, 9*(1), 24–43.

Hauser, C., Tappenier, G., & Walde, J. (2007). The learning region: The impact of social capital and weak ties on innovatio. *Regional Studies, 41*(1), 75–88.

Hill, P. C., & Pargament, K. I. (2008). Advances in the conceptualization and measurement of religion and spirituality: Implications for physical and mental health research. *American psychologist* 58.1: 64.

Hughes, M., Morgan, R. E., Ireland, R. D., & Hughes, P. (2011). Network behaviours, social capital, and organisational learning in high-growth entrepreneurial firms. *International Journal of Entrepreneurship and Small Business, 12*(3), 257–272.

Hughes, M., Morgan, R. E., Ireland, R. D., & Hughes, P. (2014). Social capital and learning advantages: A problem of absorptive Capacity. *Strategic Entrepreneurship Journal, 8*(3), 214–233.

Inkpen, A. C., & Tsang, E. W. K. (2005). Social capital, networks, and knowledge transfer. *Academy of Management Review, 30*(1), 146–165.

Kambil, A., Eselius, E. D., & Monteiro, K. A. (2000). Fast venturing: The quick way to start web businesses. *Sloan Management Review, 41*(4), 55–68.

Lane, P. J., & Lubatkin, M. (1998). Relative absorptive capacity and inter-organizational learning. *Strategic Management Journal, 19*(5), 461–477.

Laursen, K., Masciarelli, F., & Prencipe, A. (2012a). Regions matter: How localized social capital affects innovation and external knowledge acquisition. *Organization Science, 23*(1), 177–193.

Laursen, K., Masciarelli, F., & Prencipe, A. (2012b). Trapped or spurred by the home region? The effects of potential social capital on involvement in foreign markets for goods and technology. *Journal of International Business Studies, 43*, 783–807.

Lavie, D. (2006). The competitive advantage of interconnected firms: An extension of the resource-based view. *Academy of Management Review, 31*(3), 638–658.

Lazoi, M., Ceci, F., Corallo, A., & Secundo, G. (2011). Collaboration in an aerospace SMEs cluster: Innovation and ict dynamics. *International Journal of Innovation and Technology Management, 8*(3), 393–414.

Lim, C., & Putnam, R. D. (2010). Religion, social networks, and life satisfaction. *American Sociological Review, 75*(6), 914–933.

Madhok, A., & Tallman, S. B. (1998). Resources, transactions and rents: Managing value through interfirm collaborative relationships. *Organization Science, 9*(3), 326–339.

Maine, E., Soh, P.-H., & Dos Santos, N. (2015). The role of entrepreneurial decision-making in opportunity creation and recognition. *Technovation, 39*, 53–72.

Meyer, J., Becker, T., & Van Dick, R. (2007). Social identities and commitments at work: Toward an integrative model. *Journal of Organizational*

78   *Applications*

Behavior: The International Journal of Industrial, Occupational and Organizational Psychology and Behavior 27: 665–683.

Nahapiet, J., & Ghoshal, S. (1998). Social capital, intellectual capital, and the organizational advantage. *Academy of Management Review, 23*(2), 242–266.

Neubert, M. J., Bradley, S. W., Ardianti, R., & Simiyu, E. M. (2017). The role of spiritual capital in innovation and performance: Evidence from developing economies. *Entrepreneurship Theory and Practice, 41*(4), 621–640.

Oppenheim, A. V. (2000). *Questionnaire design, interviewing and attitude measurement*. London: Pinter.

Perry-Smith, J. E., & Mannucci, P. V. (2017). From creativity to innovation: The social network drivers of the four phases of the idea journey. *Academy of Management Review, 42*(1), 53–79.

Putnam, R D. (1993). The prosperous community: Social capital and public life. *The American Prospect, 13*(4), 35–42.

Putnam, R D. (2000). *Bowling alone*. Palgrave Macmillan, New York.

Putnam, R. D, Campbell, D. E., & Garrett, S. R. (2012). *American grace: How religion divides and unites us*. New York: Simon and Schuster.

Rietveld, C. A., & Van Burg, E. (2014). Religious beliefs and entrepreneurship among Dutch protestants. *International Journal of Entrepreneurship and Small Business, 23*(3), 279–295.

Ringle, C. M., Wende, S., & Becker, J.-M. (2015). SmartPLS 3. SmartPLS GmbH, Boenningstedt. *Journal of Service Science and Management*, 10.3

Roessingh, C., & Boersma, K. (2011). 'We are growing Belize': modernisation and organisational change in the Mennonite settlement of Spanish Lookout, Belize. *International Journal of Entrepreneurship and Small Business, 14*(2), 171–189.

Roessingh, C., & Nuijten, M. (2012). Female self-employment among the Kleine Gemeinde in the Mennonite settlement of Blue Creek, Northern Belize. *International Journal of Entrepreneurship and Small Business, 15*(4), 397–410.

Rogers, E. M. (2010). *Diffusion of innovations*. New York: Simon and Schuster.

Sarkar, M., Cavusgil, S. T., & Evirgen, C. (1997). A commitment-trust mediated framework of international collaborative venture performance. *Cooperative Strategies: North American Perspectives, 1*, 255–285.

Saxenian, A. (1994). *Regional advantage: Culture and competition in silicon valley and route 128*. Cambridge, MA: Harvard University Press.

Schulz, M. (2001). The uncertain relevance of newness: Organizational learning and knowledge flows. *Academy of Management Journal, 44*(4), 661–681.

Smith, C., Smith, J. B., & Shaw, E. (2017). Embracing digital networks: Entrepreneurs' social capital online. *Journal of Business Venturing, 32*(1), 18–34.

Sorenson, O., Rivkin, J. W., & Fleming, L. (2006). Complexity, networks and knowledge flow. *Research Policy, 35*(7), 994–1017.

Spear, R. (2010). Religion and social entrepreneurship. *Values and opportunities in social entrepreneurship*. Palgrave Macmillan, London. pp. 31–51.

Swedberg, R. (2000). *Entrepreneurship: The social science view* (Vol. 1). Oxford: Oxford University Press.

Tajfel, H., & Turner, J. C. (2004). The social identity theory of intergroup behavior. *Psychology of Intergroup Relations* 2: 7–24.

Tsai, W., & Ghoshal, S. (1998). Social capital and value creation: The role of intrafirm networks. *Academy of Management Journal, 41*(4), 464–476.

Vissa, B. (2012). Agency in action: Entrepreneurs' networking style and initiation of economic exchange. *Organization Science, 23*(2), 492–510.

Weber, M. (1904). *Die protestantische Ethik und der Geist des Kapitalismus.* CH Beck.

Wiesenfeld, B. M., Raghuram, S., & Garud, R. (2001). Organizational identification among virtual workers: The role of need for affiliation and perceived work-based social support. *Journal of Management, 27*(2), 213–229.

Williams, D. (2006). On and off the'Net: Scales for social capital in an online era. *Journal of Computer-Mediated Communication, 11*(2), 593–628.

Woolcock, M., & Narayan, D. (2000). Social capital: Implications for development theory, research, and policy. *The World Bank Research Observer, 15*(2), 225–249.

Yli-Renko, H., Autio, A., & Sapienza, H. J. (2001). Social capital, knowledge acquisition, and knowledge exploitation in young technology-based firms. *Strategic Management Journal, 22*(6–7), 587–613.

5 Cultural Proximity within Organizations
Evidences from Teams

Introduction

In this chapter, we present an individual social value evaluation model, known as social axioms (Leung & Bond, 2004), to investigate how cultural proximity affects team performance. As extensively discussed in Chapter 2, Leung, Bond, Reimel de Carrasquel, Muñoz, Hernández, & Murakami (2002) defined social axioms as *"generalized beliefs about oneself, the social and physical environment, or the spiritual world, [stated] in the form of an assertion about the relationship between two entities or concepts."* The concept of social axiom is intended to offer a cognitive interpretation of the way individuals relate to others and their environment, as well as examining the relevance of beliefs in different social contexts (Leung, Bhagat, Buchan, Erez, & Gibson, 2005; Leung & Bond, 2004; Leung et al., 2002).

Teams can offer a directed and collaborative effort to address complex tasks, therefore organizations have significantly increased their dependency on teams (Montoya-Weiss, Massey, & Song, 2001; Salas, Dickinson, Converse, & Tannenbaum, 1992). Over the years, teamwork has been the subject of a number of definition attempts (Katzenbach & Smith, 1993) and classify teams (Cohen & Bailey, 1997; Dunphy & Bryant, 1996). Teamwork involves interdependent behaviors of team members that translate inputs (e.g. capabilities, materials, resources) into outputs (e.g. products, services) (Marks, Mathieu, & Zaccaro, 2001). Organizing work in teams grants access to a broader array of perspectives, capabilities, and efforts. The configuration of team members' attributes, termed team composition, has a major influence on teamwork: team composition affects team performance and outcome (Levine, 1990; Salas, Cooke, & Rosen, 2008). With the increase in the adoption of teamwork, these early ideas evolved and were applied to understanding its effectiveness (Mann, 1959).

Prior studies have analyzed the effects of team members' characteristics on team performance. Research focused on the demographic characteristics within a team, in terms of age difference (Gellert & Kuipers, 2008; Wegge, Roth, Neubach, Schmidt, & Kanfer, 2008), work experience (Tihanyi, Ellstrand, Daily, & Dalton, 2000), gender diversity (Bell, Villado, Lukasik, Belau, & Briggs, 2011; Herring, 2009), team size (Haleblian & Finkelstein, 1993), virtual team (Kirkman & Gibson, 2004; Prasad & Akhilesh, 2002), and national diversity (Hofstede, 2011). Members of demographically diversified teams are likely to have greater differences in their view of team goals: it is therefore possible to agree on the importance of team design as a way of aligning team's composition with organizational objectives and resources (Kozlowski & Ilgen, 2006). A further key factor relates to the personal characteristics of each team member, such as leadership (Cohen & Bailey, 1997; Srivastava, Bartol, & Locke, 2006), goal orientation (Porter, 2005), creativity (Bouncken, Brem, & Kraus, 2016), communication (Matveev & Nelson, 2004), and social values (Drach-Zahavy, 2004; Ng & Sears, 2012). These studies have shown how team members' personality determines team performance (Kichuk & Wiesner, 1997). However, only a few studies have examined the sharing of social values among team members, despite the fact that, at the stage of team building, the analysis of cultural proximity within the team is essential.

Based on the research on the expectancy-value theory, this chapter investigates the role of cultural proximity in terms of shared value within the team as well as its effects on team performance. This is accomplished by operationalizing the concept of cultural proximity leveraging upon the contribution of Leung et al (2002): the construct of social axioms defining cultural dimensions as the identifying beliefs of the world in which each individual lives and works has been adopted. Social axioms may be described as individual evaluations and beliefs about the social context constraining and influencing individual behavioral choices. Accordingly, based on the above definition and the impact of cultural diversity in team performance, we propose the following research questions: *Does cultural proximity in terms of shared values between team members affect team performance?*

We posited that cultural proximity and social value of each team member influenced team performance and the degree of "homogeneity" of their group context would have an impact on team performance. On an empirical level, this chapter relies on primary survey data from 56 teams and 376 team members. Our findings add to a better understanding of the multifaceted nature teams that illustrate how team performance is influenced by cultural proximity.

Theoretical Framework

The focus of research on teams remains strong due to the importance of collaborative processes to organization performance (Hoegl & Proserpio, 2004). To cope with the growing complexity of the environment, organizations are increasingly turning to team-based structures (Katzenbach & Smith, 1993; Salas, Sims, & Burke, 2005). In the context provided in this chapter, teams are defined as a group of two or more individuals who have specified roles and who adaptively, interdependently, and dynamically interact to achieve a common and valued goal (Dyer, 1984; Salas et al., 2005) According to previous studies, team members require the ability to coordinate tasks and cooperatively interact with each other through a shared understanding of team resources (e.g. knowledge, skills, and experiences of members), team goals and objectives, and the constraints influencing the way the team works (Bowers, Braun, & Morgan Jr, 1997, p. 90). Teams also require teamwork. It can be referred to as a set of interrelated actions, thoughts, and feelings of each team member that are necessary for the team to function (e.g. Salas et al., 2005).

With the increase in team deployment, research attention on the prediction of effective team performance and the variables that may promote or detract from team performance has also increased (Hackman, 1980). Proximity among team members has been widely investigated (Hoegl & Proserpio, 2004): a seminal work by Allen (1970) puts the concept of proximity in relation to that of physical distance, measured in terms of feet or meters. This measure proposed by Allen is dyadic since it refers to pairs of individuals. As opposed to this, in this chapter, we will focus on the team level rather than the dyadic level due to our requirement of a team-level concept of proximity. Furthermore, our interest is in the distance from a cognitive rather than a physical point of view. Therefore, we rely on the concept of cultural proximity using the construct of social axioms proposed by Leung et al. (2002). Social axioms are people's beliefs about the way the world functions and they provide a different type of general orientation (Leung et al., 2002) These general beliefs about the world are likely to affect behaviors across different contexts (Leung et al., 2002). When making a decision, people apply what they know about the world (Furnham, 1988). This knowledge provides a personal representation that people develop over the course of their life experiences. According to

Leung et al. (2002), what people know about the world is a predictor value for determining their behavior. Based on qualitative research and the literature on beliefs, Leung et al. (2002) developed a social axiom survey. Using this survey, they identified the following five factors of beliefs: (i) reward for application is the assumption that an investment in human resources will result in positive outcomes (e.g. 'Hard working people will achieve more in the end'); (ii) social cynicism is a negative evaluation of social events and human nature (e.g. 'Kind-hearted people usually suffer losses'); (iii) social complexity is the view that there are multiple solutions to social issues, and that the outcome of events is indeterminate (e.g. 'One has to deal with matters according to the specific circumstances'); (iv) fate control is a general belief that external forces influence social events (e.g. 'Fate determines one's successes and failures'); and, ultimately, (v) spirituality is the view that spiritual forces have an impact on the human world (e.g. 'Religious people are more likely to maintain moral standards'). These five dimensions and their defining items have been identified in 40 countries.

Research Methods

To examine the relationship between team performance and team cultural proximity primary survey data have been used. The data collection process was conducted among students enrolled in BA and Master course in Management, and a total of 378 complete questionnaires has been collected. The questionnaire was administered to the students who participated in the project work, which represented an important part of their final exam. Students were asked to collaborate in an organized and creative way to develop a solution to a business problem. The types of solutions required ranged from creating a startup, to identifying a marketing strategy, to planning a project for the development of a new product. The data cover a three-year period from 2015–2016 to the academic year 2017–2018, and data on 56 teams were collected.

The questionnaire was structured in 4 main sections. The first section collected personal information regarding the age, gender, nationality, education, and work experiences of respondents. The second section asked questions on the relationship with other group members in terms of information exchange and frequency of the relationship. The third section assessed self-reported answers for the dependent variables, namely the perceived performance of the group. Ultimately, the fourth section collected information in terms of individual culture and beliefs employing the items of social axioms. Table 5.3A in the Appendix provides a detailed list of those items. The questionnaire has been distributed to English-speaking and Italian-speaking students. The data has been collected in Italy, although the questionnaire had been prepared in 2 languages: Italian and English for foreign students. To check the accuracy of the translation, a back translation technique was applied (Leung et al., 2002). To increase the response rate, we guaranteed confidentiality and confirmed that that data would be used only for academic purposes. The questionnaire is included in the Appendix. On average, the individuals in our sample are 25 years old and come from 13 different European countries. Female respondents account for 56% of the sample.

Dependent variable. Our dependent variable is *Team performance expectation* and it refers to the expectation of team members on the final performance of the team.

Independent variables. Cultural proximity in the team was operationalized using the 1- Herfindahl's index of social axioms reflecting cultural proximity among team members. Specifically, *Reward for Applications proximity, Fate Control proximity, Social cynicism proximity, Social complexity proximity, Religiosity proximity* were included in the model.

Control variables. Indicators that investigate member characteristics and teamwork composition were adopted as control variables. Variables describing the demographic composition of the group were included in the model, such as: (i) *Age,* measured as the average age of team members, and (ii) *Gender,* a dummy variable which takes the value of 1 if all the members of the group are of the same gender; otherwise, it takes the value of 0. Prior experiences of group members were also controlled by including in the model: (i) *Work experience,* a dummy variable that takes the value of 1 if at least one member of the team has any previous working experience, otherwise it takes the value of 0, and (ii) *Startup,* a dummy variable that takes the value of 1 if at least one member of the team is the founder of a startup, otherwise it takes the value of 0.

An ordinary least squares (OLS) model was employed to examine the effects of the different forms of cultural proximity on the expected team performance. Table 5.1 shows the correlation between the variables and the *main* descriptive statistics. No major collinearity issues are detectable. In order to assess potential multicollinearity, the variance inflation factors (VIFs) were computed. For each model (see Table 5.2), the mean and maximum VIF are well below the thresholds of 6 and 10, respectively. We thus concluded that multicollinearity does not pose a threat to the validity of our results.

Table 5.1 Correlation matrix

	Mean	SD	1	2	3	4	5	6	7	8	9
1 Team performance expectation	-1.83e-09	0.362	–								
2 Reward_prox	-2.044	3.612	-0.271	–							
3 Fatecontrol_prox	-1.297	1.944	0.169	-0.012	–						
4 Socialcynism_prox	-2.271	2.709	0.352	-0.093	-0.5703	–					
5 Socialcomplesity_prox	-1.885	3.227	-0.109	-0.254	-0.1589	-0.062	–				
6 Religiosity_prox	-1.767	2.246	-0.129	-0.104	-0.3109	-0.035	-0.429	–			
7 Age	32.307	53.385	0.123	-0.051	-0.1078	-0.166	0.015	-0.118	–		
8 Startup	0.160	0.370	-0.126	0.167	0.1218	0.053	0.037	0.094	0.049	–	
9 Work Experience	0.892	0.312	-0.132	0.155	0.1142	0.193	-0.050	-0.005	-0.054	-0.151	–
10 Gender	0.446	0.501	-0.068	0.296	-0.2206	-0.017	0.133	0.219	0.124	0.099	0.153

Table 5.2 Moderate regression analysis

	Model 1			Model 2			Model 3			Model 4			Model 5			Model 6		
	Coeff.	Std. Error		Coeff.	Std. Error		Coeff.	Std. Error		Coeff.	Std. Error		Coeff.	Std. Error		Coeff.	Std. Error	
Reward_prox	-0.040	0.013	**													-0.043	0.013	**
Fatecontrol_prox				0.029	0.026											0.015	0.031	
Socialcynism_prox							0.043	0.018	*							0.0411	0.021	*
Socialcomplesity_prox										-0.013	0.015					0.003	0.015	
Religiosity_prox													-0.029	0.022		-0.036	0.024	
Age	-0.001	0.001		-0.001	0.001		0.001	0.001		-0.001	0.001		-0.001	0.001		-0.001	0.001	
Work experience	0.175	0.128		0.093	0.135		0.101	0.129		0.113	0.136		0.126	0.135		0.191	0.122	
Startup	0.243	0.153		0.143	0.161		0.082	0.157		0.152	0.162		0.161	0.607		0.176	0.148	
Gender	0.161	0.099		0.086	0.103		0.063	0.096		0.073	0.102		0.091	0.102		0.216	0.102	*
R^2	0.149			0.055			0.151			0.041			0.051			0.333		
Model F	10.760			0.714			10.780			0.420			0.540			0.018		
N	56			56			56			56			56			56		

a *Significant at the 0.10 level. **Significant at the 0.05 level. **Significant at the 0.01 level.

Findings, Value, and Implication

Our results (Table 5.2, Model 1.1) suggest that *Reward for Applications proximity* has a negative effect on the expected team performance. As described above, people who exhibit high levels of reward for application believe that hard work and effort will be rewarded in the long term (Leung & Bond, 2004). Reward for application largely focuses on the self or one's personal efforts in relation to the desired outcomes. On the other hand, Model 1.3 suggests that *Social Cynicism proximity* has a positive effect on the dependent variable. These results show that cultural proximity between group members is related to the performance of the group itself, albeit in a different manner: teams having a heterogeneous composition in terms of reward for application are more likely to achieve success in terms of team performance. In contrast, a heterogeneous composition in terms of social cynicism has a negative impact on team performance. The remaining independent variables are not significant in explaining *Team performance expectation.*

Explaining whether and how the personal beliefs of individual team members affect the composition of the team itself is of great interest to both scholars and practitioners to understand why some teams are more productive than others (Bell, 2007; Groves & Feyerherm, 2011; Kirkman & Shapiro, 2005; Pieterse, Van Knippenberg, & Van Dierendonck, 2013).

This chapter was intended to further advance the research on team performance, exploring the interaction between cultural proximity in terms of individual beliefs and team results. Our findings show that changes in cultural proximity (measured in terms of social axioms) between the members of the group are related to the performance of the group itself. For example, our results indicated that *reward for application* and *social cynicism* are related to the results of team performance. This chapter provides an important theoretical contribution as it bridges the gap in the literature that investigates the relationship between cultural proximity and team performance. Research in the field of organization studies has called for studies that take into account contingencies of the effects of cultural diversity on teams (Pelled, Eisenhardt, & Xin, 1999; Van Knippenberg & Mell, 2016). We thus answer to this call by focusing on team cultural proximity and building on the differences in cultural values between team members. Our results suggest that cultural proximity between group members is related to the performance of the group itself, although the influence varies depending on the type of cultural values. In some cases, in fact, heterogeneity is positive, while being negative in others. This has some practical implications for both management and entrepreneurs. Team organization is extremely important for any business, as teams play a key role in the goal orientation of every firm. Through the operationalization of values, achieved by using social axiom constructs, it is possible to analyze and understand the norms of cultural compatibility, group identity, and creativity between members of the same group. This implies that managers may develop a team goal of cultural compatibility based on the type of group they are working for.

This study is, of course, not devoid of limitations. First, we only considered a sample of students while future research could be replicated in different organizational contexts. Second, while these students are from 13 different countries, data have only been collected in Italian Universities. Future studies could benefit from an expansion in different countries to understand whether national culture plays a role in affecting the relationship between cultural proximity and group performance. Finally, our dataset only includes 56 final teams. Future studies could test our predictions on a larger sample of teams.

References

Allen, T. J. (1970). Communication networks in R & D Laboratories. *R&D Management, 1*(1), 14–21.

Bell, S. T. (2007). Deep-level composition variables as predictors of team performance: A meta-analysis. *Journal of Applied Psychology, 92*(3), 595–615.

Bell, S. T., Villado, A. J., Lukasik, M. A., Belau, L., & Briggs, A. L. (2011). Getting specific about demographic diversity variable and team performance relationships: A meta-analysis. *Journal of Management, 37*(3), 709–743.

Bouncken, R., Brem, A., & Kraus, S. (2016). Multi-cultural teams as sources for creativity and innovation: The role of cultural diversity on team performance. *International Journal of Innovation Management, 20*; 1650012-1650045

Bowers, C. A., Braun, C. C., & Morgan Jr, B. B. (1997). Team workload: Its meaning and measurement. In Brannick M.T, Salas E. & Prince C.W. (Eds.) *Team performance assessment and measurement* (pp. 97–120). New York: Psychology Press.

Cohen, S. G., & Bailey, D. E. (1997). What makes teams work: Group effectiveness research from the shop floor to the executive suite. *Journal of Management, 23*, 239–290.

Drach-Zahavy, A. (2004). Exploring team support: The role of team's design, values, and leader's support. *Group Dynamics, 8*(4), 235–252.

Dunphy, D., & Bryant, B. (1996). Teams: Panaceas or prescriptions for improved performance? *Human Relations, 49*(5), 677–699.

Dyer, J. L. (1984). Team research and team training: A state-of-the-art review. *Human Factors Review, 26*, 285–323.

Gellert, F. J., & Kuipers, B. S. (2008). Short- and long-term consequences of age in work teams. *Career Development International, 13*(2), 132–149.

Groves, K. S., & Feyerherm, A. E. (2011). Leader cultural intelligence in context: Testing the moderating effects of team cultural diversity on leader and team performance. *Group and Organization Management, 36*(5), 535–566.

Hackman, J. R. (1980). Work redesign and motivation. *Professional Psychology: Research and Practice, 11*(3), 445–455.

Haleblian, J., & Finkelstein, S. (1993). Top Management team size, CEO dominance, and firm performance: The moderating roles of environmental turbulence and discretion. *Academy of Management Journal, 36*, 844–863.

Herring, C. (2009). Does diversity pay?: Race, gender, and the business case for diversity. *American Sociological Review, 74*(2), 208–224.

Hoegl, M., & Proserpio, L. (2004). Team member proximity and teamwork in innovative projects. *Research Policy, 33*(8), 1153–1165.

Hofstede, G. (2011). Dimensionalizing cultures: The hofstede model in context. *Online Readings in Psychology and Culture, 2*, 8.

Katzenbach, J., & Smith, D. K. (1993). *The wisdom of teams. Greating the high performance organisation.* Boston, MA: Harvard Business School Press. McKinsey & Company.

Kichuk, S. L., & Wiesner, W. H. (1997). The big five personality factors and team performance: Implications for selecting successful product design teams. *Journal of Engineering and Technology Management - JET-M, 14*(3), 195–221.

Kirkman, B. L., & Gibson, C. B. (2004). The impact of team empowerment on virtual team performance: The moderating role of face-to-face interaction. *Academy of Management Journal, 47*(2), 175–192.

Kirkman, B. L., & Shapiro, D. L. (2005). The impact of cultural value diversity on multicultural team performance. *Advances in International Management, 18*(3), 33–67.

Kozlowski, S. W. J., & Ilgen, D. R. (2006). Enhancing the efectiveness of work groups and teams. *Psychological Science in the Public Interest, Supplement, 7*(3), 77–124.

Leung, K., Bhagat, R. S., Buchan, N. R., Erez, M., & Gibson, C. B. (2005). Culture and international business: Recent advances and their implications for future research. *Journal of International Business Studies, 36*(4), 357–378.

Leung, K., & Bond, M. H. (2004). Social Axioms: A Model for Social Beliefs in Multicultural Perspective. In M. P. Zanna (Ed.), *Advances in experimental social psychology* (Vol. 36, pp. 119–197). Elsevier Academic Press.

Leung, K., Bond, M. H., Reimel de Carrasquel, S., Muñoz, C., Hernández, M., & Murakami, F. (2002). Social axioms: The search for universal dimensions of general beliefs about how the world functions. *Journal of Cross- Cultural Psychology, 33,* 286–302.

Levine, J. (1990). Progress In Small Group Research. *Annual Review of Psychology, 41,* 585–634.

Mann, R. D. (1959). A review of the relationships between personality and performance in small groups. *Psychological Bulletin, 66,* 241–270.

Marks, M. A., Mathieu, J. E., & Zaccaro, S. J. (2001). A temporally based framework and taxonomy of team processes. *Academy of Management Review, 26*(3), 356–376.

Matveev, A. V., & Nelson, P. E. (2004). Cross cultural communication competence and multicultural team performance: Perceptions of American and Russian managers. *International Journal of Cross Cultural Management, 4,* 253–270.

Montoya-Weiss, M. M., Massey, A. P., & Song, M. (2001). Getting it together: Temporal coordination and conflict management in global virtual teams. *Academy of Management Journal, 44*(6): 1251–1262.

Ng, E. S., & Sears, G. J. (2012). CEO leadership styles and the implementation of organizational diversity practices: Moderating effects of social values and age. *Journal of Business Ethics, 105*(1), 41–52.

Pelled, L. H., Eisenhardt, K. M., & Xin, K. R. (1999). Exploring the black box: An analysis of work group diversity, conflict, and performance. *Administrative Science Quarterly, 44*(1), 1–28.

Pieterse, A. N., Van Knippenberg, D., & Van Dierendonck, D. (2013). Cultural diversity and team performance: The role of team member goal orientation. *Academy of Management Journal, 56*(3), 782–804.

Porter, C. O. L. H. (2005). Goal orientation: Effects on backing up behavior, performance, efficacy, and commitment in teams. *Journal of Applied Psychology, 90*(4), 811–818.

Prasad, K., & Akhilesh, K. B. (2002). Global virtual teams: What impacts their design and performance? *Team Performance Management: An International Journal, 8*(5/6), 102–112.

Salas, E., Cooke, N. J., & Rosen, M. A. (2008). On teams, teamwork, and team performance: Discoveries and developments. *Human Factors, 50*(3), 540–547.

Salas, E, Dickinson, T. L., Converse, S. A., & Tannenbaum, S. I. (1992). Toward an understanding of team performance and training. In Swezey R: W. & Salas E. (Eds.), *Teams: Their training and performance* (pp. 3–29). Ablex Publishing.

Salas, E., Sims, D. E., & Burke, C. S. (2005). Is there a "big five" in teamwork? *Small Group Research, 36*(5), 555–599.

Srivastava, A., Bartol, K. M., & Locke, E. A. (2006). Empowering leadership in management teams: Effects on knowledge sharing, efficacy, and performance. *Academy of Management Journal, 49*(6), 1239–1251.

Tihanyi, L., Ellstrand, A. E., Daily, C. M., & Dalton, D. R. (2000). Composition of the top management team and firm international diversification. *Journal of Management, 26*(6), 1157–1177.

Van Knippenberg, D., & Mell, J. N. (2016). Past, present, and potential future of team diversity research: From compositional diversity to emergent diversity. *Organizational Behavior and Human Decision Processes, 136*, 135–145.

Wegge, J., Roth, C., Neubach, B., Schmidt, K. H., & Kanfer, R. (2008). Age and gender diversity as determinants of performance and health in a public organization: The role of task complexity and group size. *Journal of Applied Psychology, 93*, 1301–1313.

Appendix

Table 5.3A Detailed list of items

	Min	Max	Mean	SD
Personal data – education and work experience				
Undergraduate/graduate studies	0	1	0.429	0.429
Work experience	0	1	0.982	0.312
Start-up	0	1	0.161	0.371
Group and project Characteristics				
Group Size	2	5	3.750	1.195
Gender	0	1	0.464	0.538
Group performance				
We work together	1	5	1.800	0.406
There is group concern for quality performance	1	5	1.800	0.516
we share high performance expectation	1	5	1.663	0.546
Some take our group work too lightly	1	5	3.126	0.719
Sane team members with a good idea don't speak up	1	5	4.021	0.516
Some member of the group would not disagree for fear of what others might think	1	5	3.916	0.678
Some team member act like they know it all	1	5	3.642	0.8085
One or two members tend to dominate the discussion	1	5	3.242	0.840
We listen to each individual's input	1	5	1.558	0.474
Team members feel free to make positive or negative comments	1	5	1.495	0.349
An atmosphere of trust exists in our group	1	5	1.758	0.350
We are comfortable in the roles we play in the group	1	5	1.726	0.458

Social Axiom	Loading	Alpha
Reward for application		
The just will eventually defeat the wicked	0.547	0.357
Adversity can be overcome by effort	0.477	0.328
Every problem has a solution	0.608	0.243
Knowledge is necessary for success	0.591	0.452
Caution helps avoid mistakes	0.303	0.144
Significant achievement requires one to show no concern for the means needed for that achievement	0.485	0.288
Failure is the beginning of success	0.698	0.120
One will succeed if he/she really tries	0.333	0.305
One who does know to plan his or her future will eventually fail	0.625	0.322
Hard-working people will achieve more in the end	0.070	0.153
Social justice can be maintained if everyone cares about politics	0.416	0.551
A modest person can make a good impression on people	0.243	0.289
Good deeds will be rewarded, and bad deeds will be punished	0.452	0.364
Competition brings about progress	0.395	0.190
Mutual tolerance can lead to satisfactory human relationships	0.215	0.213
Fate Control		
Fate determines one's successes and failures	0.477	0.033
Good luck follows if one survives a disaster	0.386	0.191
A person's talents are inborn	0.014	0.476
All things in the universe have been determined	0.318	0.595
Most disasters can be predicted	0.243	0.282
There are certain ways to help us improve our luck and avoid unlucky things	0.205	0.122
Individual characteristics, such as appearance and birthday, affect one's fate	0.218	0.322
Social Cynicism		
Most people hope to be repaid after they help others	0.315	0.327
Harsh laws can make people obey	0.153	0.419
Kind-hearted people usually suffer losses	0.302	0.807
The various social institutions in society are biased toward the rich	0.488	0.429
Old people are a heavy burden on society	0.444	0.294
Old people are usually stubborn and biased	0.613	0.223
People deeply in love are usually blind	0.643	0.347
Humility is dishonesty	0.177	0.421
Power and status make people arrogant	0.527	0.178
People will stop working hard after they secure a comfortable life	0.497	0.304

(Continued)

Social Axiom	Loading	Alpha
It is easier to succeed if one knows how to take shortcuts	0.249	0.277
Young people are impulsive and unreliable	0.668	0.629
Powerful people tend to exploit others	0.542	0.227
Religion makes people escape from reality	0.114	0.401
Kind-hearted people are easily bullied	0.436	0.431
Females need a better appearance than males	0.265	0.216
Ghosts or spirits are people's fantasy	0.297	0.214
To care about societal affairs only brings trouble for yourself	0.304	0.500
It is rare to see a happy ending in real life	0.266	0.244
Religious beliefs lead to unscientific thinking	−0.158	0.360
Social complexity		
Human behavior changes with the social context	0.638	0.441
To deal with things in a flexible way leads to success	0.616	0.184
There is usually only one way to solve a problem	−0.271	0.113
To plan for possible mistakes will result in fewer obstacles	0.263	0.118
One has to deal with matters according to the specific circumstances	0.384	0.192
There are phenomena in the world that cannot be explained by science	0.200	0.149
To experience various lifestyles is a way to enjoy life	0.494	0.532
Current losses are not necessarily bad for one's long-term future	0.307	0.179
Individual effort makes little difference in the outcome	−0.539	0.322
One's appearance does not reflect one's character	0.317	0.198
One's behaviors may be contrary to his or her true feelings	0.673	0.424
People may have opposite behaviors on different occasions	0.676	0.261
Religiosity		
Religious people are more likely to maintain moral standards	0.475	0.382
There is a supreme being controlling the universe	0.634	0.276
Belief in a religion makes people good citizens	0.735	0.297
Belief in a religion helps one understand the meaning of life	0.804	0.264
There are many ways for people to predict what will happen in the future	0.254	0.117
Religious faith contributes to good mental health	0.791	0.146

6 The Evolution of Proximity

The Impact of the Digital Revolution

Introduction

Recent technological innovations in ICT are giving rise to a new paradigm shift in industry, resulting in the emergence of the so-called "intelligent factory" or "industry 4.0" (Brettel, Friederichsen, Keller, & Rosenberg, 2014; Posada et al., 2015). This revolution involves, in the first place, the human capital that will be transformed into the skills possessed and enriched with new skills. In 2007, Bartel, Ichniowski, and Shaw had already observed how every investment in ICT coincided with an increase in the skill requirements of operators, with particular reference to technical skills and problem-solving. The relationship between people and business is changing: it will be necessary to reconcile the academic knowledge with the practice of 'learning by doing,' thus integrating the world of school, university, and training with that of the business. This synergy will help to respond to the greater demand for high levels of skills sought by the factories in the future.

Additionally, this new paradigm will also have another characteristic: the fall of the space-time limits of work. The flexibility introduced by the smart factory, along with the diffusion of IoT (Internet of things) technologies, allows the reorganization of work. The spatial and temporal boundaries of the latter are thus changing, thereby enabling remote production control and in some cases making the physical presence of the worker at the production site superfluous, promoting innovative forms of work organization such as smart working. Therefore, following the requirements of the digital revolution, people have started to adopt different tools to communicate, cooperate, and be connected with various actors, suppliers, and customers. They employ a wide array of ICT technologies to share knowledge and information. These technologies include internet of things and services, ubiquitous information, visual computing, intelligent robotics, product lifecycle management, cyber physical systems, cloud computing, and others (Posada et al., 2015; Prezioso, Ceci, & Za, 2020). These technologies have led to the emergence of smart manufacturing, and they are strongly catalyzing the manufacturing industry (Camarinha-Matos, Fornasiero, & Afsarmanesh, 2017; McEwan, 2016). E-mail, video conferencing, virtual communities, and other tools can be used to connect with other people. For example, the design process when using virtual technologies is both easier and cheaper (Faems, Janssens, Madhok, & Looy, 2008; Hardwick, Anderson, & Cruickshank, 2013). The use of ICT in firms as a means to support innovation is widely recognized in the literature (Levy, Loebbecke, & Powell, 2003; Zhu, 2004). The use of ICT in firms has been claimed to potentially reduce transaction and coordination costs, thus increasing the value of transactions. ICT is seen as an important tool to communicate, to enhance external communication, to reduce inefficiencies, and to accelerate the communication process. The creation of innovation and knowledge occurs through an interactive, iterative, network-based process (Konsti-Laakso, Pihkala, & Kraus, 2012).

In the innovation process, ICT is deemed essential to ensure high levels of interaction, connection, and sharing between different actors. ICT can be used to support and aid interactions and the generation of new ideas, communication, and dissemination of information, along with the creation and sharing of knowledge between the different nodes of the network. Collaborative technologies create a new space where information is distributed and made available to each actor. This new space features wide access (i.e. the possibility to access everywhere), large scale (i.e. a large amount of information and its elaboration), distribution cognition and intelligence (i.e. the information is distributed across actors, space and time), and invisible computing (i.e. the difference between the digital and real world is not visible) (Carley, 2000). The rest of the chapter discusses three different aspects of the relationship between ICT-based interactions and innovative activities, paying specific attention to the role played by cultural proximity.

The Use of Digital Tools to Enhance Proximity in Innovation Activities

The first case is built on the work by Ceci, Lazoi, Mohammad, and Corallo (2019). This work was intended to explore how ICT and face-to-face relationships take place in an innovative context and the circumstances under which physical and cultural proximity can be overcome by the use of ICT tools. Innovation has been widely studied in association with the importance of face-to-face interactions (Acs & Varga, 2002; Brown & Duguid, 2001; McCann, 2007; Nonaka & Takeuchi, 1995; Saxenian, 1994). Krugman (1991) suggests that a face-to-face contact will improve the possibilities for informal dissemination of knowledge between firms and individuals; as a result, these face-to-face contacts will promote innovation. Hardwick, Cruickshank and Anderson (2012) observed that firms rely more on face-to-face interactions for innovation, despite the adoption of one of the most widespread ICT technologies. The authors conducted a case study on an Italian SME working in the field of design, development, and manufacturing of aerospace components. The firm is a first-level supplier, collaborating with its customers to satisfy their technological needs; it also collaborates with second-level suppliers and other actors, such as universities and research centers. It is therefore responsible for the management of a large network of partners, suppliers, and customers. To better illustrate the context of the aerospace industry, one interviewee said:

> The aircraft design is done by the network. The design is distributed among global firms. Moreover, for the engine, the same paradigm applies (...) It is not a classical supply chain relationship (...) risks are shared. Therefore, the relationships inside the aerospace industry are not simply customer-supplier relationships. They are, in fact, more complex due to the network environment.

The research was intended to investigate the role played by different types of interaction (ICT, face-to-face, other device-based) in supporting innovation activities. We explored this issue by using content analysis. More specifically, we investigated how different concepts overlap in the speech and mind of the respondents. The analysis leads to significant results: the role of face-to-face interaction is more prominent in innovative activities as compared to strategic and operative activities.

The results suggest that the impact of the various communication tools is different depending on the type of activity: face-to-face interactions are more widely used in the early stages of innovation. Due to the complex nature of innovation, organizations need to share their resources with each other and cooperate to enhance their innovative activities. The connections between actors foster innovation processes, as their ideas and resources can be creatively combined. Empirical observations highlight that a change in the frequency of face-to-face interactions is a feature subject to variations in every sector. The use of ICT in firms as a means to support innovation is widely recognized in the literature (Levy et al., 2003; Zhu, 2004). It has been argued that the use of ICT in firms will reduce transaction and coordination costs, thus increasing the value of transactions. ICT is seen as an important tool to communicate, enhance external communication, reduce inefficiencies, and accelerate the communication process. In the innovation process, ICT is considered essential to ensure high levels of interaction, connection, and sharing between different actors. ICT can be used to support and facilitate interaction and generation of new ideas, communication, and dissemination of information, along with the creation and sharing of knowledge between the various nodes of the network.

"Follow-The-Sun" Method and the Overcoming of Cultural Barriers

The "follow the sun" method refers to the practice of leaving work unfinished, usually software-related, and passing it from one site to another, generally on a daily basis. This practice allows the development of a software with a 24-hour coverage, increasing the speed of development as the work takes place in all shifts (Carmel, Dubinsky, & Espinosa, 2009; Carmel, Espinosa, & Dubinsky, 2010). During an interview conducted by one of the authors of the book, an interviewee from a software house described its participation in a project applying the "follow the sun" method as follows:

> as early as 2011 we agreed to participate in a very ambitious program for the development of a coding methodology distributed in the various time zones. The project was called "24 hours" and wanted to apply the so-called "follow the sun" method, that is, a cycle of continuous development that shifted the moment of development to the countries that at that moment, due to the different time zones, were active. So, the work started in Japan, then the Japanese went to sleep, we wake up and we go back to work where they left off. So, imagine an extremely complex scenario because it is one thing to develop artifacts, let's say where it is possible to actually get to a certain point and give control to another, an account is to develop in

the software, then work of ingenuity, then enter the same line of thinking of other people in other countries. Nobody, to tell the truth, were particularly enthusiastic about participating in such a project, but we agreed to participate and it was then a success that allowed us to gain international visibility which has continued over the years with another series of projects.

The main problems encountered were related to the difficulties in work coordination between people having a similar technical background but completely different cultures. Other challenges were linked to the loss of communication richness that can only be obtained via face-to-face communication (see above); asynchronous communication, language differences, and the management of religious or national holidays.

The first documented experience of the "follow the sun" method was developed by IBM in 1997 (Carmel, 1999). In order to achieve this goal, five teams were created in five different countries. The main coordination problems emerged especially during the daily handover. These problems were so significant that the project leader abandoned the use of "follow the sun" method. However, the method was further implemented in IBM by improving the methodology. Treinen and Miller-Frost (2006) give details of two additional case studies at IBM. Their goal was to understand how to create a development environment where the "follow the sun" method could enable teams to work during local business hours and, at the end of their day, pass their tasks to teams that had just started their day. They examined a case of failure and a case of success, and then considered the factors influencing the outcome of their respective projects. The study on the case of success describes a software project involving development sites in the US and Australia: two geographically distant development groups were merged into one cohesive team for the 'follow the sun' development. The study on the case of failure involved three distinct projects located in the US and India. Unfortunately, since the design team had never worked with the remote team in India, the specifications given during the design phase were often based on assumptions that could easily be misinterpreted by the remote team. The major factor here was the loss of informal communication channels, naturally occurring in collocated teams. The loss of face-to-face communications resulted in a loss of trust between the members of the distributed teams (Calefato & Lanubile, 2016; Lanubile, Damian, & Oppenheimer, 2003; Treinen & Miller-Frost, 2006). In this case, soft skills related to social interaction proved to be more relevant than technical skills. Obviously, culture played a crucial role. As the authors state:

> Given that the two teams came from opposite sides of the globe (i.e. US and Australia), culture was something that required special attention. Because both teams came from English-speaking countries, it might have been assumed that culture would play a minimal role in our success. In truth, cultural understanding was something that had to be practiced by both teams. For example, a comment intended as a small joke could potentially derail the project if it were misunderstood as an insult.
>
> (Treinen & Miller-Frost, 2006, p. 777)

Treinen and Miller-Frost (2006) also reported that cultural diversity resulted in difficulties in forming a sense of camaraderie. Treinen and Miller-Frost (2006) also state:

> Often, the remote teams were very polite and did not ask many questions. When asked if they had a good understanding of the requirements and if they would be able to meet a scheduled date for a task, the answer was often yes, but the local team did not have enough cultural awareness to under- stand that the responses given by the remote team might need additional probing. Another issue was respect for the holidays and work week of the remote team. (...) They expected the remote teams to be available at all hours regardless of holidays or typical work weeks, which was not always possible. This eroded the team relationships even further.
>
> (Treinen and Miller-Frost, 2006, p. 780)

In line with this reasoning, Kroll, Hess, Audy, and Prikladnicki (2011) and Kroll, Richardson, Prikladnicki and Audy (2018) show that cultural challenges are associated with the cultural diversity present in "follow the sun" development environments. This diversity is comprised of social, ethnic, and cultural aspects (Jabangwe & Nurdiani, 2010; Jiménez, Piattini, & Vizcaíno, 2009), and the common problems of supporting collaboration are exacerbated by language and diversity (Cameron, 2004). Kroll et al. (2011) state

> if one culture has more emphasis on self-sufficiency, therefore they tend not to ask for help when problems come up. Another culture would not offer their help unless they were asked while

the third considered that presenting the problem was a sufficient invitation for willing team members to jump in and help
(Kroll et al., 2011, p. 4)

Cultural differences often create misunderstandings and lead to
frustration and conflicts between teams (Yap, 2005).

In order to address this issue, Treinen and Miller-Frost (2006)
suggest the inclusion of face-to-face kickoff meetings, frequent face-
to-face meetings between team leaders, the adoption of tools to re-
activate informal communications, and a greater cultural awareness
for teams. Furthermore, the training for cultural awareness conducted at the launch of the project proves to be useful for team members to understand and respect the various differences in working
styles and schedules. Cultural diversity has been shown to be a crucial aspect deserving special attention, and it must be addressed with
sensitivity; otherwise, the breakdown of relationships will compro-
mise the success of the project. Therefore, cognition or knowledge
about different cultures, motivation to interact with other cultures,
and a communicative behavior that adapts to different cultures has
proven to be a key ability for the improvement of performance in
globally distributed teams (Henderson, Stackman, & Lindekilde,
2018; Kroll et al., 2018; Presbitero & Toledano, 2018).

The Creation of Cultural Proximity within Online
Communities in Virtual Spaces

Digitalization and the growing interconnection between distant
countries and places have allowed the flourishing of communities that meet, interact, exchange ideas, create products, and give
rise to political movements (Benjamin, Zhang, Nunamaker, &
Chen, 2016; Dahlander, Frederiksen, & Rullani, 2008; Jeppesen &
Frederiksen, 2006; O'Mahony & Lakhani, 2011; Tsai & Bagozzi,
2014). Virtual communities differ from traditional communities in
the absence of physical proximity: interactions take place online
and the individuals who compose them hardly have encounters in
reality. They are also ephemeral as they can easily be exhausted
after the conversation on a given topic is saturated, and the individuals who compose them may even lie about their identity and actual
degree of involvement in such a topic. Online, everyone can build
their own relational network based on their interests and values.
Some sociologists maintain that it is not appropriate to consider
online communities as real communities mainly because of the

absence of physical proximity and also because, being connected online, there is no possibility to really share the consequences and responsibilities as one would normally do in a traditional community (Driskell & Lyon, 2002; Wellman & Gulia, 1999). However, the impact of these communities is widely studied, and they play an increasingly important role in fostering innovation, generating knowledge, and contributing to the design and govern of online activities (Dahlander et al., 2008; Faraj, Jarvenpaa, & Majchrzak, 2011; O'Mahony & Ferraro, 2007; West & O'mahony, 2008).

One example is represented by the online communities that have generated and presently manage the Online Black Markets (OBMs) existing in the Dark Net. As defined by Bartlett (2014), the Dark Net is a peculiar mixture of crime and idealism, including dissident sites and drug markets, terrorism, and many other things, and it should be thoroughly looked at as a global phenomenon. The OBMs consist of digital platforms and complementary technologies that connect buyers and vendors interested in the exchange of specific goods, mainly illegal products and services. Although initially promoted as an emancipation tool to support idealistic whistle-blowers in eluding traffic analysis for marketing purposes and Internet surveillance in oppressive regimes, in recent years, the Dark Net has been paving the way for various forms of illegal activities, such as money laundering and drug trafficking. The Dark Net is characterized by adverse conditions and it operates in the absence of formal rules, law enforcement control, legal protection, and social legitimacy for the actors involved in this ecosystem (Beckert & Wehinger, 2013; Ceci, Prencipe, & Spagnoletti, 2018; Paquet-Clouston, Décary-Hétu, & Morselli, 2018). Therefore, these actors are forced to constantly rethink their activities and innovate their products and coordination patterns (Kraemer-Mbula, Tang, & Rush, 2013).

A considerable amount of literature has focused on DNMs user practices with the aim of exploring the ways OBMs operate (Bakken, Moeller, & Sandberg, 2017; Hazel Kwon, Shakarian, Priniski, Sarkar, & Shakarian, 2017; Van Hout & Bingham, 2014; Kethineni, Cao, & Dodge, 2017; Lacson & Jones, 2016; Wehinger, 2011). Evidence shows how community members manage to coordinate by communicating anonymously via Tor messaging and forums to build trust and collectively solve problems (e.g. Lacson & Jones, 2016). In fact, the activity of online communities plays a key role in allowing the platform to function appropriately (Bakken et al., 2017; Holt, Strumsky, Smirnova, & Kilger, 2016; Markopoulos, Dimitris, & Chrysanthos, 2016; Odabas, Holt, & Breiger, 2017; Spagnoletti, Ceci, & Bygstad, 2018). Online communities are represented by hackers who provide services for the operation of the OBMs, by users who review and evaluate the platforms, thus contributing to the generation of knowledge about how the OBMs ecosystem works (Tzanetakis, Kamphausen, Werse, & von Laufenberg, 2016; Yannikos, Schäfer, & Steinebach, 2018). Actors experience various trust issues: moral hazard issues arise when vendors receive payment without providing the requested products, or when platform administrators take the money and suddenly close the market, through a fraudulent practice called "exit scam" (Bhaskar, Linacre, & Machin, 2017); vendors are exposed to the risk of imprisonment when they trade illicit goods with undercover police officers. Lack of trust can have serious consequences on the survival of an OBM. To address these problems, OBM admins regulate transactions by rating vendors, banning deceivers, and providing escrow services to suspend payments until all parties are satisfied (Bakken et al., 2017; Odabas et al., 2017). Additionally, Masson and Bancroft (2018) observed that OBMs are not perfect, but their operation is strongly influenced by the role of some communities negotiating drug use and supply. Therefore, through collective efforts to build trust and create a "safe" system in the absence of formal rules and control, the creation of a common culture within the community is thus established. Cultural proximity is the key to dispute resolution and the proper functioning of online markets. As reported by Maddox, Barratt, Allen, and Lenton (2016), in forums,

> participants discussed harnessing and developing the technological tools needed to access Silk Road (i.e. one of the first OBM platforms to appear on the DarkNet) and engage within the Silk Road community. For participants Silk Road was not just a market for trading drugs: it facilitated a shared experience of personal freedom within a libertarian philosophical framework, where open discussions about stigmatized behaviours were encouraged and supported.
>
> (Maddox et al., 2016, p. 111)

Similarly, Maddox et al. (2016) add:

> Participants who had been active on Silk Road since its launch reported that there was initially a high level of technical skill needed, which effectively limited access to the site and the community, creating a small techno-elite who in their shared interest in such sophisticated computer use became a unique and supportive community culture.
>
> (Maddox et al., 2016, p. 116)

References

Acs, Z. J., & Varga, A. (2002). Geography, endogenous growth, and innovation. *International Regional Science Review, 25*(1), 132–148.

Bakken, S. A. A., Moeller, K., & Sandberg, S. (2017). Coordination problems in cryptomarkets: Changes in cooperation, competition and valuation. *European Journal of Criminology, 15*(2), 442–460.

Bartlett, J. (2014). *The dark net: Inside the digital underworld.* New York, Melville House

Beckert, J., & Wehinger, F. (2013). In the shadow: Illegal markets and economic sociology. *Socio-Economic Review, 11*, 5–30.

Benjamin, V., Zhang, B., Nunamaker, J. F., & Chen, H. (2016). Examining hacker participation length in cybercriminal internet-relay-chat communities. *Journal of Management Information Systems, 33*(2), 482–510.

Bhaskar, V., Linacre, R., & Machin, S. (2017). The economic functioning of online drugs markets. *Journal of Economic Behavior and Organization, 159*(C), 426–441.

Brettel, M., Friederichsen, N., Keller, M., & Rosenberg, M. (2014). How virtualization, decentralization and network building change the manufacturing landscape: An industry 4.0 perspective. *International Journal of Mechanical, Industrial Science and Engineering, 8*(1), 37–44.

Brown, J. S., & Duguid, P. (2001). Knowledge and organization: A social-practice perspective. *Organization Science, 12*(2), 198–213.

Calefato, F., & Lanubile, F. (2016). Affective trust as a predictor of successful collaboration in distributed software projects. *2016 IEEE/ACM 1st International Workshop on Emotional Awareness in Software Engineering (SEmotion)* (pp. 3–5). New Jersey, USA IEEE.

Camarinha-Matos, L. M., Fornasiero, R., & Afsarmanesh, H. (2017). Collaborative networks as a core enabler of industry 4.0. 2017 *Working Conference on Virtual Enterprises* (pp. 3–17). Cham, Springer

Cameron, A. (2004). A novel approach to distributed concurrent software development using a follow-the-sun technique. *Unpublished EDS Working Paper.*

Carley, K. M. (2000). Computational analysis of social and organizational systems. *Organizational Science, 34*(2), 4–10.

Carmel, E. (1999). *Global software teams: Collaborating across borders and time zones.* London, Prentice Hall PTR.

Carmel, E., Dubinsky, Y., & Espinosa, A. (2009). Follow the sun software development: New perspectives, conceptual foundation, and exploratory field study. *2009 42nd Hawaii International Conference on System Sciences* (pp. 1–9). New Jersey, USA: IEEE.

Carmel, E., Espinosa, A. J., & Dubinsky, Y. (2010). 'Follow the sun' workflow in global software development. *Journal of Management Information Systems, 27*(1), 17–38.

Ceci, F., Lazoi, M., Mohammad, H., & Corallo, A. (2019). Collaborative relationships strengthening innovative activities: An industrial exploration. *European Conference on Intangibles and Intellectual Capital* (pp. 67–X). Italy, Academic Conferences International Limited.

Ceci, F., Prencipe, A., & Spagnoletti, P. (2018). Evolution, resilience and organizational morphing in anonymous online marketplaces. *AOM Specialized Conference, Big Data and Managing in a Digital Economy* (pp. 18–20). April, Guilford, UK.

Dahlander, L., Frederiksen, L., & Rullani, F. (2008). Online communities and open innovation. *Industry and Innovation, 15*(2), 115–123.

Driskell, R. B., & Lyon, L. (2002). Are virtual communities true communities? Examining the environments and elements of community. *City & Community, 1*(4), 373–390.

Faems, D., Janssens, M., Madhok, A., & Looy, B. V. (2008). Toward an integrative perspective on alliance governance: Connecting contract design, trust dynamics, and contract application. *The Academy of Management Journal, 51*(6), 1053–1078.

Faraj, S., Jarvenpaa, S. L., & Majchrzak, A. (2011). Knowledge collaboration in online communities. *Organization Science, 22*(5), 1224–1239.

Hardwick, J., Anderson, A. R., & Cruickshank, D. (2013). Trust formation processes in innovative collaborations: Networking as knowledge building practices. *European Journal of Innovation Management, 16*(1), 4–21.

Hardwick, J., Cruickshank, D., & Anderson, A. R. (2012). Innovation in small business: Comparing face-to-face with virtual networking. *Journal of Business Strategy, 33*(5), 51–58.

Hazel Kwon, K., Shakarian, J., Priniski, J. H., Sarkar, S., & Shakarian, P. (2017). Crisis and collective problem solving in dark web: An exploration of a black hat forum. *Proceedings of the 8th International Conference on Social Media & Society - #SMSociety17* (pp. 1–5). Vol. Part F1296. New York, USA: Association for Computing Machinery.

Henderson, L., Stackman, R., & Lindekilde, R. (2018). Why cultural intelligence matters on global project teams. *International Journal of Project Management, 36*, 954–967.

Holt, T. J., Strumsky, D., Smirnova, O., & Kilger, M. (2016). Examining the social networks of malware writers and hackers. *International Journal of Cyber Criminology, 6*, April, 891–903.

Van Hout, M. C., & Bingham, T. (2014). Responsible vendors, intelligent consumers: Silk road, the online revolution in drug trading. *International Journal of Drug Policy, 25*(2), 183–189.

Jabangwe, R., & Nurdiani, I. (2010). Global software development challenges and mitigation strategies: A systematic review and survey results. Master Thesis, Blekinge Institute of Technology, Thesis No: MSE-2010-13, 2010.

Jeppesen, L. B., & Frederiksen, L. (2006). Why do users contribute to firm-hosted user communities? The case of computer-controlled music instruments. *Organization Science, 17*(1), 45–63.

106 *Applications*

Jiménez, M., Piattini, M., & Vizcaíno, A. (2009). Challenges and improvements in distributed software development: A systematic review. *Advances in Software Engineering.* 710971

Kethineni, S., Cao, Y., & Dodge, C. (2017). Use of bitcoin in darknet markets: Examining facilitative factors on bitcoin-related crimes. *American Journal of Criminal Justice,* 43(2), 141–157.

Konsti-Laakso, S., Pihkala, T., & Kraus, S. (2012). Facilitating SME innovation capability through business networking. *Creativity and Innovation Management, 21*(1), 93–105.

Kraemer-Mbula, E., Tang, P., & Rush, H. (2013). The cybercrime ecosystem: Online innovation in the shadows? *Technological Forecasting and Social Change, 80*(3), 541–555.

Kroll, J., Hess, E. R., Audy, J. L. N., & Prikladnicki, R. (2011). *Researching into follow-the-sun software development: Challenges and opportunities.* In 2011 *IEEE Sixth International Conference on Global Software Engineering,* August, 60–65. IEEE.

Kroll, J., Richardson, I., Prikladnicki, R., & Audy, J. L. N. (2018). "Empirical evidence in follow the sun software development: A systematic mapping study. *Information and Software Technology, 93,* 30–44.

Krugman, P. R. (1991). *Geography and trade.* Cambridge, MA. The MIT Press.

Lacson, W., & Jones, B. (2016). The 21st century dark net market: Lessons from the fall of silk road. *International Journal of Cyber Criminology, 10*(1), 40–61.

Lanubile, F., Damian, D., & Oppenheimer, H. L. (2003). Global software development: Technical, organizational, and social challenges. *ACM SIGSOFT Software Engineering Notes, 28*(6), 2.

Levy, M., Loebbecke, C., & Powell, P. (2003). SMEs, co-opetition and knowledge sharing: The role of information systems1. *European Journal of Information Systems, 12*(1), 3–17.

Maddox, A., Barratt, M. J., Allen, M., & Lenton, S. (2016). Constructive activism in the dark web: Cryptomarkets and illicit drugs in the digital 'demimonde.' *Information, Communication & Society, 19*(1), 111–126.

Markopoulos, P., Dimitris, X., & Chrysanthos, D. (2016). Manipulating reviews in dark net markets to reduce crime. *Conference on Information Systems and Technology,* Philadelphia, PA.

Masson, K., & Bancroft, A. (2018). 'Nice people doing shady things': Drugs and the morality of exchange in the darknet cryptomarkets. *International Journal of Drug Policy, 58,* 78–84.

McCann, P. (2007). Sketching out a model of innovation, face-to-face interaction and economic geography. *Spatial Economic Analysis, 2*(2), 117–134.

McEwan, A. M. (2016). *Smart working: Creating the next wave.* New York, Routledge.

Nonaka, I., & Takeuchi, H. (1995). *The knowledge-creating company.* New York: Oxford University Press.

Odabas, M., Holt, T. J., & Breiger, R. L. (2017). Governance in online illicit stolen data mar- kets. In J. Beckert & M. Dewey (Eds.), *The architecture of illegal markets.* Cambridge, England: Oxford University Press.

O'Mahony, S., & Ferraro, F. (2007). The emergence of governance in an open source community. *Academy of Management Journal, 50*(5), 1079–1106.

O'Mahony, S., & Lakhani, K. R. (2011). Organizations in the shadow of communities. *Communities and organizations,* 33, 3–36.

Paquet-Clouston, M., Décary-Hétu, D., & Morselli, C. (2018). Assessing market competition and vendors' size and scope on AlphaBay." *International Journal of Drug Policy, 54,* 87–98.

Posada, J., Toro, C., Barandiaran, I., Oyarzun, D., Stricker, D., de Amicis, R., Pinto, E. B., Eisert, P., Döllner, J., & Vallarino, I. (2015). Visual computing as a key enabling technology for industrie 4.0 and industrial internet. *IEEE Computer Graphics and Applications, 35*(2), 26–40.

Presbitero, A., & Toledano, L. S. (2018). Global team members' performance and the roles of cross-cultural training, cultural intelligence, and contact intensity: The case of global teams in IT offshoring sector. *The International Journal of Human Resource Management, 29*(14), 2188–2208.

Prezioso, G., Ceci, F., & Za, S. (2020). Employee skills and digital transformation: preliminary insights from a case study. *Impresa Progetto.* 2, 1–23

Saxenian, A. (1994). *Regional advantage: Culture and competition in silicon valley and route 128.* Cambridge, MA: Harvard University Press.

Spagnoletti, P., Ceci, F., & Bygstad, B. (2018). An investigation on the generative mechanisms of Dark Net markets. *WISP 2018 Proceedings.* 20.

Treinen, J. J., & Miller-Frost, S. L. (2006). Following the sun: Case studies in global software development. *IBM Systems Journal, 45*(4), 773–783.

Tsai, H. T., & Bagozzi, R. P. (2014). Contribution behavior in virtual communities: Cognitive, emotional, and social influences. *Mis Quarterly, 38*(1), 143–164.

Tzanetakis, M., Kamphausen, G., Werse, B., & von Laufenberg, R. (2016). The transparency paradox. Building trust, resolving disputes and optimising logistics on conventional and online drugs markets. *International Journal of Drug Policy, 35,* 58–68.

Wehinger, F. (2011). The dark net: Self-regulation dynamics of illegal online markets for identities and related services. *2011 European Intelligence and Security Informatics Conference* (pp. 209–213). New Jersey, USA, IEEE.

Wellman, B., & Gulia, M. (1999). Virtual communities as communities. In M. A. Smith & P. Kollock (Eds.), *Communities in cyberspace* (pp. 167–194). London: Routledge.

West, J., & O'mahony, S. (2008). The role of participation architecture in growing sponsored open source communities. *Industry and Innovation, 15*(2), 145–168.

Yannikos, Y., Schäfer, A., & Steinebach, M. (2018). Monitoring Product Sales in Darknet Shops. *Proceedings of the 13th International Conference on Availability, Reliability and Security*, August: 1–7.

Yap, M. (2005). Follow the sun: Distributed extreme programming development. *Agile Development Conference (ADC'05)* (pp. 218–224). New Jersey, USA: IEEE.

Zhu, K. (2004). The complementarity of information technology infrastructure and e-commerce capability: A resource-based assessment of their business value. *Journal of Management Information Systems, 21*(1), 167–202.

Conclusions

The present work explores the role and implications of culture diversity and cultural proximity within organizations. In this chapter, our aim was to provide a global view of the phenomenon. We have opened the black box of cultural proximity, that is, shared language, codes, communication norms, and exchange between actors, investigating the different aspects of cultural diversity and its role as a catalyst or obstacle within innovation processes. We did so on the basis of original empirical evidences from surveys and case studies, and through multiple theoretical approaches from a variety of fields (i.e. sociology, management, and economy). In the following sections, we will look at the implications and contributions arising from this work. The primary research findings are structured around three main subjects: (i) a theoretical exploration of the notions of cultural proximity and cultural diversity, obtained by employing different theoretical lenses, (ii) suggestions on ways to design tools and methods to enhance the role of cultural diversity as an important catalyst for innovation, and (iii) a discussion on the challenges and opportunities that cultural diversity entails.

Primary Research Findings

Subject 1: Exploring the Notions of Cultural Proximity and Cultural Diversity

In the investigation of the notion of cultural proximity and cultural diversity, a variety of theoretical approaches, such as social capital, social identity theory, cultural values, and social axioms, have been employed.

The approach of social capital has been used by exploring its conceptual foundations and empirical applications. To define social capital, we deviated from Bourdieu's (1980) definition that sees social capital as "the sum of the resources, actual or virtual, that accrue to an individual or group by virtue of possessing a durable network of more or less institutionalized relationships of mutual acquaintance and recognition" (Bourdieu, 1980, p. 2). We then examined the connections between social capital, innovation, and cultural proximity, thus elaborating on the three propositions that will be reported below. The propositions focused on (i) the role of geographical dimension, (ii) the possibility to access to localized factors, and (iii) the exchange of knowledge as influenced by the presence of different norms and rules. In summary, social capital is expected to have a different impact on different types of innovation based on cultural proximity. Therefore, in order to analyze the effect of social capital on innovation, it is important to investigate the role of cultural proximity. We argue that relating social capital with cultural proximity might help to shed light on the role of social capital in promoting firm innovation in a given geographical area. The three propositions, as developed in Chapter 1, are as follows:

Proposition 1.1: The geographical features that favor innovations are difficult to move from one place to another. These features may be pre-existing or generated by firm activities, but their access is significantly influenced by cultural proximity.

Proposition 1.2: New knowledge is generated through information and knowledge exchange among many different communities.

Proposition 1.3: The processes of creation and diffusion of innovation follow different paths. Some are essentially based on formal systems of relationship. In other cases, the exchange of knowledge and the creation of innovations cannot be controlled by means of formal procedures, but they imply trust, identification, and the respect of social norms.

The second set of lenses employed in this work includes all the studies that have identified and operationalized the concept of cultural values. More specifically, reference is made to the contribution by Hofstede (1980). Defining what we mean when we refer to culture and value is considered crucial to explore the importance of shared culture and value. We did so by drawing on the contribution of social identity theory, cultural values, and social axioms (Bond, Leung, Au, Tong, & Chemonges-Nielson, 2004; Hofstede, 1980, 2001; House, Hanges, Javidan, Dorfman, & Gupta, 2004; Leung et al., 2002; Ouchi, 1981). Specific attention was paid to the role of cultural proximity/diversity in influencing team performance. In Chapter 2, we developed the three propositions that follow:

Proposition 2.1: In teams, high levels of cultural proximity in terms of cultural compatibility predict knowledge sharing among team members thereby positively influencing team performance.

Proposition 2.2: In teams, high levels of cultural proximity in terms of identity predict knowledge sharing among team members thereby positively influencing team performance.

Proposition 2.3: In teams, high levels of cultural proximity in terms of shared norms of creativity predict knowledge sharing among team members thereby positively influencing team performance.

Subject 2: Designing Tools and Methods

This work is based on a wide range of empirical evidence originating from different industries and contexts. We have therefore identified a set of tools and methods which will be summarized as follows and can shed further light on the appropriate ways to manage diversity in order to enhance innovativeness. More specifically, our contributions focus on the following areas: (i) ICT tools and methods; (ii) entrepreneurship and start-ups; (iii) innovation process.

Regarding ICT tools and methods, in Chapter 6 we explored the role of ICT, virtual and face-to-face contacts, and their impact on innovation. Our findings suggest that ICT tools cannot replace face-to-face interaction when developing innovative projects. In fact, while ICT tools can help to overcome distance barriers and enhance productivity, cultural diversity has been found to be a critical factor that deserves special attention and needs to be addressed sensitively, otherwise relationship breakdown would jeopardize the success of the project. Therefore, knowledge and understanding of other cultures, motivation to interact with other cultures, and communication behavior that adapts to different cultures proved to be key abilities to improve performance in teams distributed throughout the world (Henderson, Stackman, & Lindekilde, 2018; Kroll et al., 2018; Presbitero & Toledano, 2018). However, under specific circumstances, digitalization and interconnection between distant countries and places have allowed the flourishing of communities that meet, interact, exchange ideas, build products, and start political movements, thus creating a shared culture that exists only in the virtual space. Although ephemeral, these communities play an increasing role in boosting innovation, generating knowledge, and contributing to the design and management of online activities (Dahlander et al., 2008; Faraj, Jarvenpaa, & Majchrzak, 2011; O'Mahony & Ferraro, 2007; West & O'mahony, 2008).

The second contribution is represented by tools and methods that refer to entrepreneurship and start-ups. From the experience presented in this book, the following lessons about the role of culture in an entrepreneurial network can be derived: (i) sharing cultural values in the network makes knowledge sharing a more natural process by enhancing trust, mutual cooperation, and solidarity, and (ii) sharing knowledge with other network members who hold fundamental values. People do not share their ideas and insights simply because it is the right thing to do. On the contrary, sharing ideas is closely related to the alignment between individuals in terms of beliefs, language, and values; (iii) networks are among the key vehicles for sharing knowledge. However, knowledge sharing also requires a culture sharing that needs to be promoted and improved by means of tools, resources, and legitimization; (iv) knowledge sharing within a network having shared cultural values has a positive effect on entrepreneurial learning. Furthermore, Chapter 5 suggests some practical implications for both management and entrepreneurs. Team organization is extremely important for every enterprise since teams play a key role in firm goal orientation. Value operationalization, achieved by the use of social axiom constructs, enables the analysis of cultural compatibility, group identity, and creativity rules between members of the same group. The implication is that managers may develop a team cultural-compatibility goal based on the type of group they are working for.

Additionally, Chapter 3 provides a set of propositions that can help the management of new technology-based ventures, that are reported below. We posit that team heterogeneity in terms of the personality of the entrepreneurial team in new technology-based ventures provides firms with a larger spectrum of perspectives which might be conducive to innovation.

Proposition 3.1: In new technology-based ventures, founders' heterogeneity in terms of personality traits promotes the development of the innovation process.

Proposition 3.2a: In new technology-based ventures, the internal social capital of the founders' team increases the proximity that exists between co-founders and promotes the implementation of an innovation.

Proposition 3.2b: In new technology-based ventures, the external social capital of the founders' team increases the heterogeneity that exists between co-founders and promotes opportunity recognition.

Finally, Chapter 4, contributes to the innovation process: social capital is confirmed to have a positive effect on the innovation process (Hauser, Tappenier, & Walde, 2007; Laursen, Masciarelli, & Prencipe, 2012; Tsai & Ghoshal, 1998), by discussing how external ties affect the innovation process and by dividing the innovation process into two distinct moments, thus showing how cultural proximity differently allows opportunity recognition and innovation implementation. This shed further light on the dynamics arising under the influence of external forces (i.e. culture, relationships, and people) on how firms organize their innovation process.

Subject 3: Understanding Challenges and Opportunities for Managers, Entrepreneurs, and Policymakers

This work also poses some challenges and identifies opportunities for entrepreneurs, managers, and policymakers. The successful management of an innovation strategy may require a careful evaluation of social relationships with external actors. Paying specific attention to managers and entrepreneurs operating in a network of firms, shared culture and shared values have been shown to have different effects on the different stages of the innovation process. Hence, professionals operating within a cultural network might be supported in achieving innovation by understanding, analyzing, and balancing cultural values and shared vision to enable innovation, entrepreneurial learning, and the accomplishment of common goals. In fact, a common view has been found to successfully promote the development of identity and shared creativity within a network. Therefore, the personal culture of the entrepreneur influences the development of his or her business, which has a significant impact on the local economic system. Due to the importance of value and culture in promoting knowledge flow, networks should include those organizations led by people who foster the culture of knowledge sharing. Our findings have also implications for policymakers. People who are responsible for the design of innovation strategies on a territorial or regional level should support the existing cultural networks in the development of the innovation process by encouraging managers and entrepreneurs to properly leverage their social capital at every stage during the innovation process.

References

Bond, M. H., Leung, K., Au, A., Tong, K. K., & Chemonges-Nielson, Z. (2004). Combining social axioms with values in predicting social behaviours. *European Journal of Personality, 18*(3), 177–191.

Bourdieu, P. (1980). Le capital social. Notes provisoires. *Actes, 31*, 2–3.

Hauser, C., Tappenier, G., & Walde, J. (2007). The learning region: The impact of social capital and weak ties on innovatio. *Regional Studies, 41*(1), 75–88.

Hofstede, G. (1980). *Culture's consequences: International differences in work-related values.* (Vol. 5). Beverly Hills, CA: Sage Publications, Incorporated.

Hofstede, G. (2001). *Culture's consequences: Comparing values, behaviors, institutions and organizations across nations.* Thousand Oaks, CA: Sage Publications.

House, R. J., Hanges, P. J., Javidan, M., Dorfman, P. W., & Gupta, V. (2004). *Culture, leadership, and organizations: The GLOBE study of 62 societies.* Thousand Oaks, CA: Sage Publications.

Laursen, K., Masciarelli, F., & Prencipe, A. (2012). Trapped or spurred by the home region? The effects of potential social capital on involvement in foreign markets for goods and technology. *Journal of International Business Studies, 43*, 783–807.

Leung, K., Bond, M. H., Reimel de Carrasquel, S., Muñoz, C., Hernández, M., & Murakami, F. (2002). Social axioms: The search for universal dimensions of general beliefs about how the world functions. *Journal of Cross- Cultural Psychology, 33*, 286–302.

Ouchi, W. G. (1981). The Z organization. *Classics of organization theory,* 451–460. New York: Avon.

Tsai, W., & Ghoshal, S. (1998). Social capital and value creation: The role of intrafirm networks. *Academy of Management Journal, 41*(4), 464–476.

About the Authors

Federica Ceci is an Associate Professor at the University G.d'Annunzio. She gained a PhD in Management Engineering at the University of San Marino (RSM). She teaches Management and Innovation in Undergraduates Programme, Corporate and University Master Courses. Her research interests include theory of the firm, management of innovation, the role of personal relationships in enabling and diffusing innovation, analysis of managerial implications of digitalization of organizational process, dynamics and organizational characteristics of the deep web, digital ecosystems and platforms. She has published, among the others, in *Research Policy, Industrial and Corporate Change, European Journal of Information Systems, Journal of International Management, Industry & Innovation, Journal of Management and Governance, European Journal of Innovation Management*. She has also published a book, *The Business of Solutions* with the Edward Elgar Publishing.

Francesca Masciarelli is an Associate Professor at the University G. d'Annunzio. She received her PhD from the University of Trento. Her research interests include entrepreneurship, social capital, strategy, and management of innovation. She published on *Organization Science, Journal of International Business Studies, Regional Studies, Industry and Innovation, Journal of Management and Governance, Sinergie, European Journal of Innovation Management, International Journal of Innovation and Technology Management*, and *Journal of Small Business and Entrepreneurship*. She has also published two books with the Edward Elgard Publishing: *The Strategic Value of Social Capital: How Firms Capitalize on Social Assets* and *Entrepreneurial Personality and Small Business Management*. She is a Senior Lecturer of Management and Entrepreneurship at the University G. d'Annunzio and LUISS University. She teaches Innovation in Corporate and University Master courses.

Index

Note: **Bold** page numbers refer to tables and *italic* page numbers refer to figures.

120   *Index*